KUSUDAMA ORIGAMI

EKATERINA LUKASHEVA

DOVER PUBLICATIONS, INC.
MINEOLA, NEW YORK

THANKS AND CREDITS

I would like to thank all my origami friends and fans, who encouraged me to write this book, especially Elena and Maria for test-folding, Tanya for the Bitterroot picture (see page 46), and most of all my beloved husband Boris, who is not only supportive, but made the website www.kusudama.me for me.

Bibliographical Note
Kusudama Origami is a new work, first published by Dover Publications, Inc., Mineola, New York, in 2014.

Library of Congress Cataloging-in-Publication Data

Lukasheva, Ekaterina.
 Kusudama origami / Ekaterina Lukasheva.
    Pages   cm
 Summary: "A kusudama is a traditional Japanese sphere formed by modular origami construction techniques. This guide presents instructions for more than forty elaborate modular origami figures that range in shape from stars to flowers to kusudama. Suitable for beginning to experienced folders of all ages"-- Provided by publisher.
 Summary: "Instructions for more than 40 kusudama origami models"-- Provided by publisher.
 ISBN-13: 978-0-486-49965-9 (pbk.)
 ISBN-10: 0-486-49965-0
 I. Title.
 TT872.5.L85 2014
 736'.982--dc23
                                                          2013035826

Manufactured in the United States by Courier Corporation
49965003   2014
www.doverpublications.com

Contents

CHAPTER 1

Farandola
✳ 2

Farandola Gemma
✳ 5

Farandola Florida
✳ 7

Farandola Granda
✳✳✳ 10

Whirlpool
✳ 13

Spaceship
✳✳ 15

Jade
✳✳ 19

Sparkling Jade
✳✳ 22

Shining Jade
✳✳✳ 24

Gem
✳✳✳✳ 25

Airy Jade
✳✳ 27

Hypnose
✳✳ 28

Coquette
✳✳ 31

CHAPTER 2

Sparaxis Flower
✻✻ 34

Sparaxis
✻✻✻ 37

Bitterroot
✻✻✻ 42

Bitterroot Variation
✻✻✻ 47

Mandragora
✻✻✻ 48

Crocus
✻✻✻ 50

Dollar Crocus
✻✻✻ 53

Dollar Sparaxis
✻✻✻ 56

Arctica
✻✻✻ 59

Lilia
✻✻✻✻ 62

Lilia Star
✻✻ 65

Mandarin
✻✻✻ 69

CHAPTER 3

Preface

This book is dedicated not only to origami enthusiasts, but to all who want to dive into the world of modular origami. If you have ever enjoyed construction sets, making paper models or puzzles, modular origami can become a wonderful new hobby for you. Give it a try!

In many ways modular origami is easier than traditional single-sheet origami. You don't need to make dozens of folds with the same sheet, only to fail at the last step. You don't need much space, because units are usually made with relatively small pieces of paper. After some practice you can even make them without a table or work surface. It's possible to create something really amazing anywhere, whether you're standing in a line at the airport or watching your favorite television show.

This book is for both children and adults. Children can discover the magic of simple three-dimensional forms made with paper, while adults can create real masterpieces. The intended audience for this book is from ages 12–99, but that doesn't mean it's impossible to teach younger children. It just means that they will likely need assistance from teachers or parents with some of the folds.

The models in the book range from super simple 15-minute projects to more complex intermediate creations.

WHAT IS ORIGAMI?

The ancient art of paper folding originated in China during the first and second centuries and reached Japan around the fourth century. The Japanese called this new form of art "origami" from the words "ori" (*to fold*) and "kami" (*paper*). During the eighth through twelfth centuries, origami played a significant role in the ceremonial life of the Japanese aristocracy. Since paper was rare and valuable, only the wealthy could afford this kind of art. The democratization of origami in Japan began between the eighteenth and nineteenth centuries, when the first books on origami were written.

China and Japan were not the only countries where people folded paper, however. Traditions of paper folding also existed in Korea, Germany, and Spain.

For many centuries the art of paper folding was taught only from one person to another. This made the spread of origami very slow. In the 1950 and 60s, Akira Yoshizawa introduced new diagramming symbols, which simplified the diagramming of the models. With some additions by Robert Harbin and Samuel Randlett, this system was adopted as the international standard for diagramming. It was no longer necessary to understand the written language, just the symbols!

Traditional origami uses a single, uncut sheet of paper. Modular origami uses two or more sheets to create the final form. Each piece of paper is folded into a unit (module) and several units are assembled to make the final shape. The units are assembled using specially created flaps and pockets, so that either tension or the structure of the folded paper holds the pieces together. Modular figures can be flat or three-dimensional. This book contains mostly three-dimensional models, as well as a few flat ones.

Modular origami has also existed for centuries, but it was not as popular as traditional origami. Its rebirth and rapid development began with the inventions of Mitsonobu Sonobe and Robert Neale in the 1960s. Since then, the genre of modular origami has become popular and extensively developed. Tomoko Fuse, a Japanese origamist, has been instrumental in the widespread popularity of modular origami. Her wonderful books on the subject have inspired many, including me.

There are various names for origami and modular origami throughout the world. In the west, the phrase "paper folding" is the most common term. In the east, "origami" is used. In Russia, where I live, we have no accepted translation for "paper folding." Perhaps this is because the words "paper" and "folding" sound too long and unpleasant in my language. The same can be said for "modular origami." While it is referred to as "modular origami" in most countries, in Russia and some other countries, the Japanese word "kusudama" is used for round modular constructions. Initially "kusudama" meant "medicine ball" in Japanese. In Japan these balls, possibly made of herbs, had been used as incense. It may not be very accurate, but most of the community uses this word. As for myself, I prefer "kusudama." Maybe I'm just the part of the community.

HOW TO BEGIN

If you are wondering where to find special origami paper, don't worry. Start with a sheet of printer paper and give it a try. You'll discover that modular origami, even made with standard printer paper, looks beautiful. All you have to do is follow the instructions, as each fold contributes to the final result.

What size paper should you use? I give some recommendations in the text, but they serve mainly for beginners. As you gain experience, you can try smaller papers. If you are teaching children, it's a good idea to start with larger sheets of paper.

Each model is marked with one to four stars. The fewer stars a model has, the easier it is. Begin with easier ones and you'll have more success. The stars mainly represent a unit's complexity. Another characteristic of the models is the number of units required. The fewer units needed, the less time you'll need to complete a model. If you are teaching children, choose models with fewer units, because it's very hard to explain to a child that thirty of those seemingly useless units will eventually form something great.

WHAT ABOUT THE PAPER?

If you are a beginner, I recommend using standard printer paper. It's advantage is that it is inexpensive, readily available, and even comes in colors.

Post-it Notes® were my favorite paper when I first started folding. They don't have to be cut for models that require square paper and you can find them at office-supply stores. If you dust the adhesive edge with starch, it will no longer be sticky.

Another readily available alternative is gift wrap. It's easy to find and comes in many colors and patterns. I would recommend kraft paper first, because it folds well and is very resilient.

Of course there is a wide range of special origami paper available. You can just search the Internet for where to purchase it. Several Internet shops sell almost every kind of paper and deliver it worldwide. Kami, Harmony or patterned paper all work well with most of the models in this book.

I should mention another thing about origami paper. The paper is either mono, which means it as the same color or design on both sides, or it is duo, meaning it has different colors on each side. Some models in this book show both sides of the paper; duo paper is recommended to make them truly beautiful.

USEFUL TOOLS

- It's very helpful to use some kind of folder for creasing. You can find specially made bone or wooden folders in craft or origami stores. Some clay modeling tools, available in art supply stores, also work well. Such folders make your creases sharp and accurate. Definitely use folders with children.

- During the assembly of the final modular, tweezers can be extremely useful. Use tweezers to tuck the flap into a pocket or for curling the petals of flowers.

- When units fall apart during the assembly, you can temporarily affix them with paper clips or fasteners. After you've assembled the figure you can remove them.

- Although the models in this book are not meant to be glued together, you may need this tool too. If you are making a present for a non-origamist or have children or pets, you may need it. It can also be helpful if you are having trouble holding together a modular for the first time. This is not a catastrophe—the skill of not using glue comes with experience.

TIPS AND TRICKS

- Choose papers of the same type and weight for a single model. Papers having various characteristics mixed in one ball can cause asymmetry or other problems.

- Before making the entire ball, try folding a test unit.

- Be as accurate as possible when making every single unit. It's not evident at first glance, but every crease contributes to the whole appearance.

- If you don't understand a step, it is helpful to look at the next picture.

ORIGAMI SYMBOLS

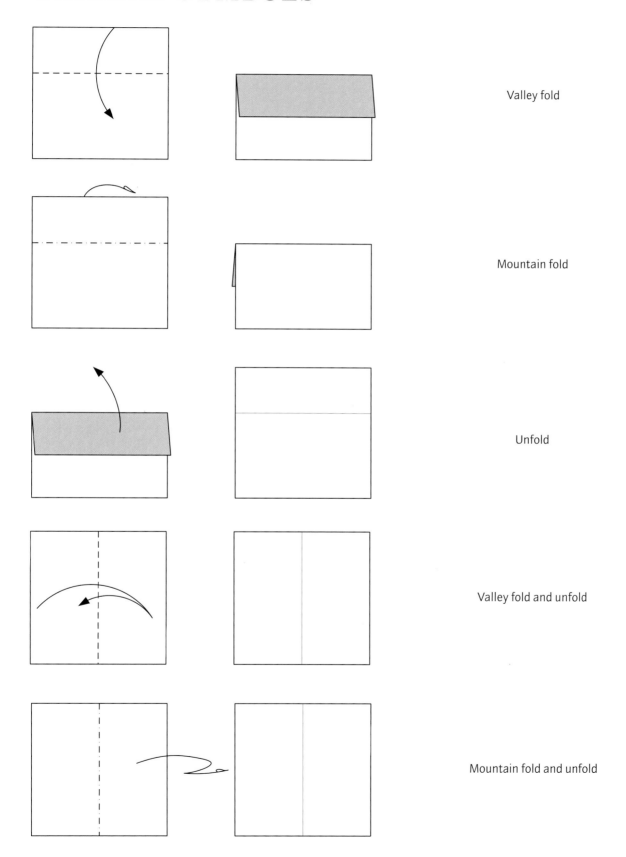

Valley fold

Mountain fold

Unfold

Valley fold and unfold

Mountain fold and unfold

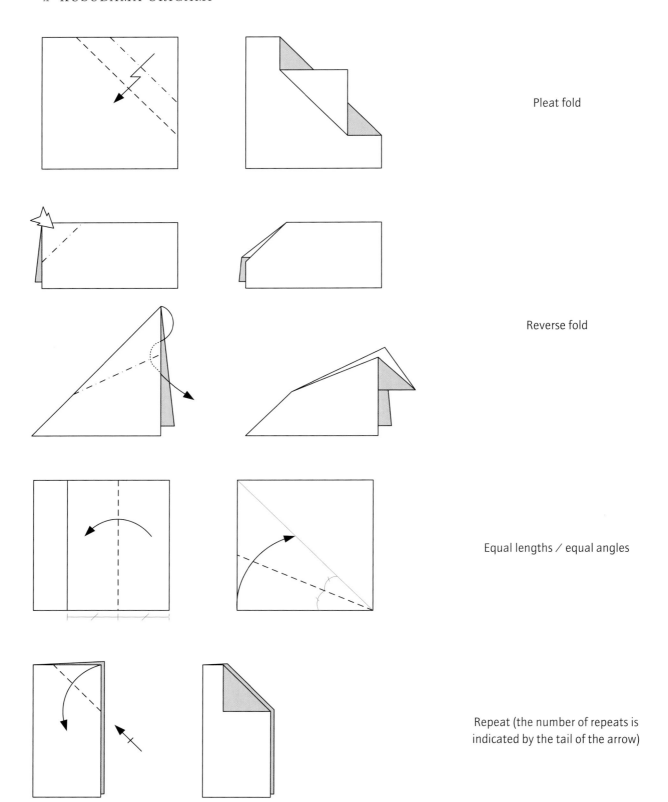

Pleat fold

Reverse fold

Equal lengths / equal angles

Repeat (the number of repeats is
indicated by the tail of the arrow)

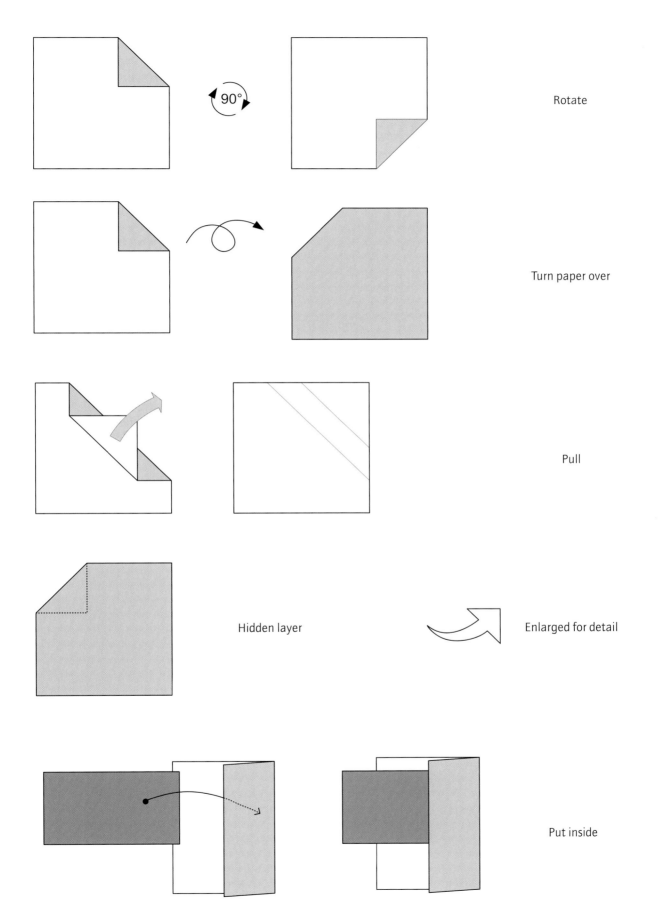

Rotate

Turn paper over

Pull

Hidden layer

Enlarged for detail

Put inside

USEFUL METHODS

How to make an A-rectangle from a square

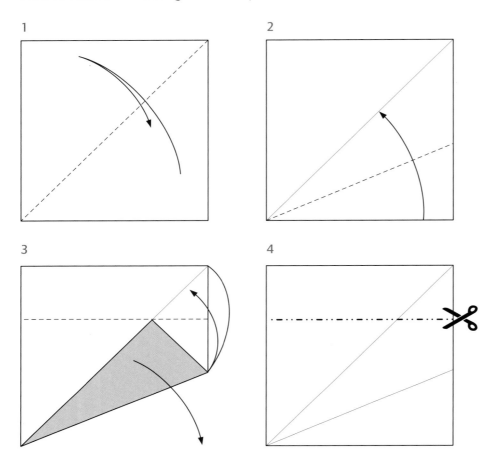

How to divide a square into 1:2 rectangles (halves)

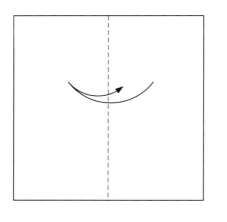
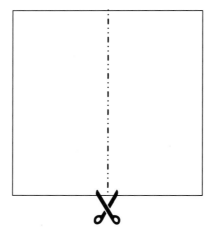

How to divide a square into thirds

1

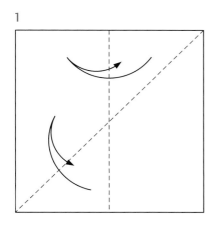

2

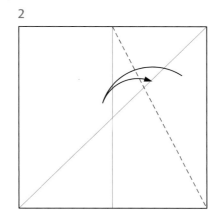

3

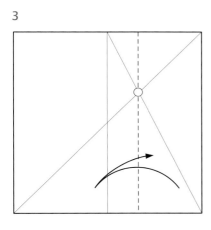

4

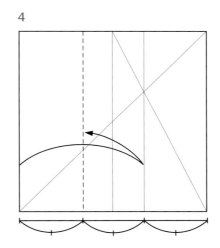

How to get 1:3 rectangles

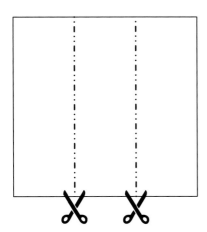

How to make 2:3 rectangles from a square.

Divide the square into thirds as shown on page xiii
and then use one of the following methods.

Method 1   *Method 2*

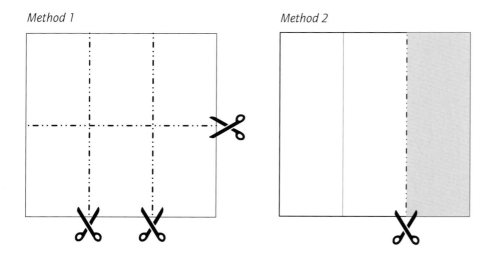

How to get banknote ($1-bill) rectangles

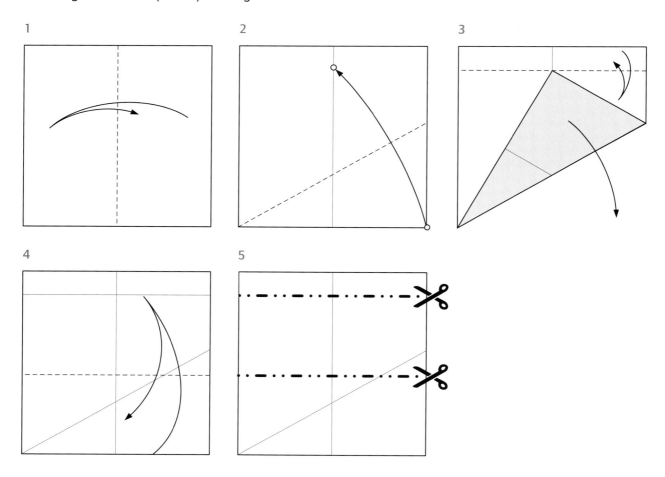

CHAPTER 1

Farandola *

PAPER: rectangular with proportions 1:2. Use rectangles that are 3 x 6 cm (1¼ x 2½ inches) or larger. See page xii for how to cut this rectangle from a square.

NUMBER OF UNITS: 12 or 30

This model is good for a beginner. Not only are the units are fast and easy to make, the edges look fascinating when curled a bit. Duo paper will work well for this model.

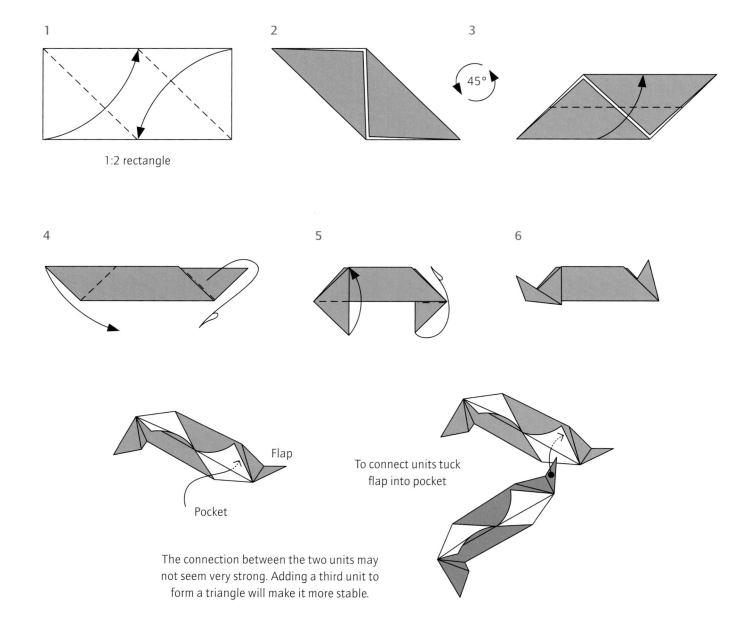

1

1:2 rectangle

2

3

45°

4

5

6

Flap

Pocket

To connect units tuck flap into pocket

The connection between the two units may not seem very strong. Adding a third unit to form a triangle will make it more stable.

12-UNIT ASSEMBLY

Depending on the paper, this type of assembly may require a little bit of glue for Farandola models.

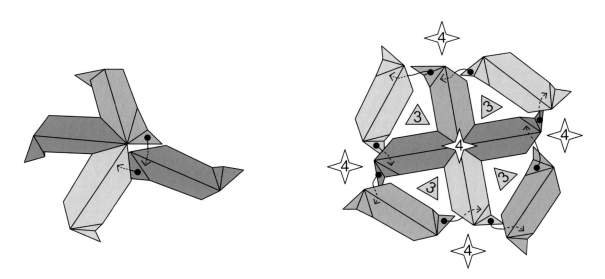

Make a star from 4 units, then connect other units so that you get
a triangle between the units each time. Continue adding units
so that 4 units meet at each point marked with a star.

30-UNIT ASSEMBLY

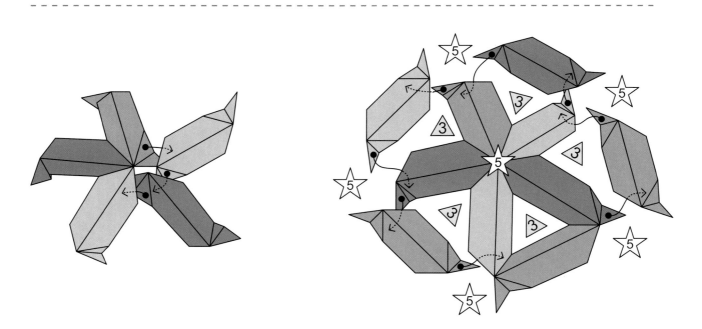

Make a star from 5 units, then connect other units so that you
get a triangle between the units each time. Continue adding
units so that 5 units meet at each point marked with a star.

Farandola Gemma *

PAPER: 6–10 cm (2¼–4 inches) square

NUMBER OF UNITS: 12 or 30

This lightweight model is decorated with tiny buds. All types of paper are suitable for this ball. Use the assembly method from page 3 for 12 units or page 4 for 30 units.

1

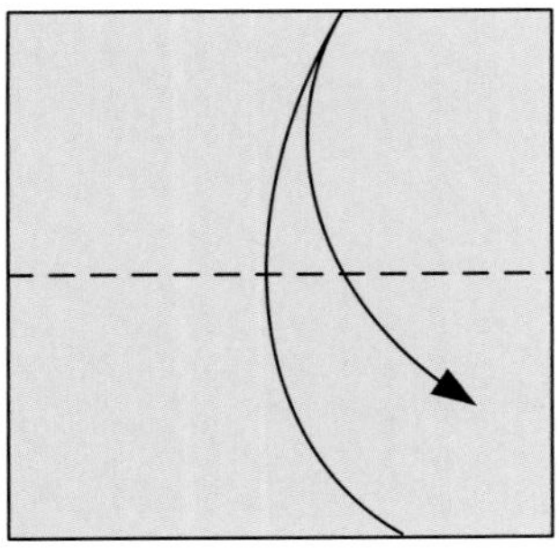

2

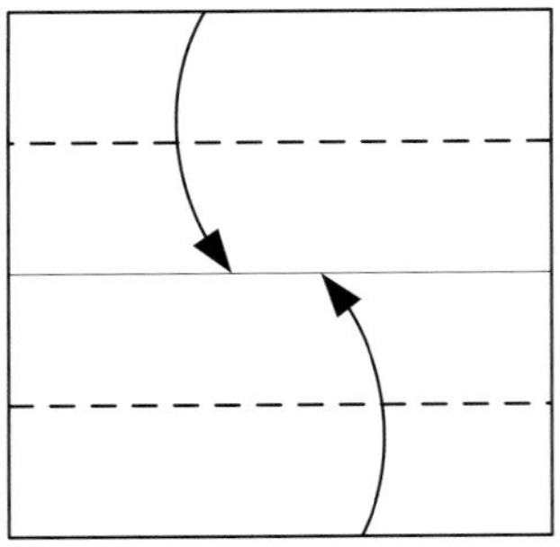

3

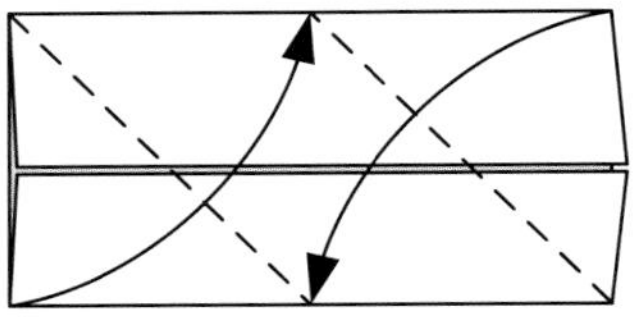

4

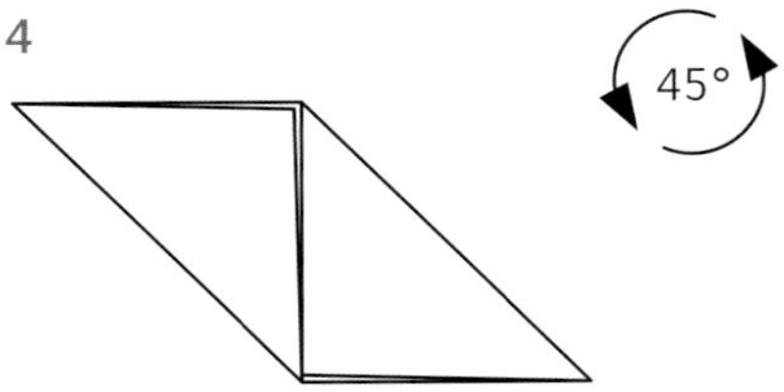

45°

5

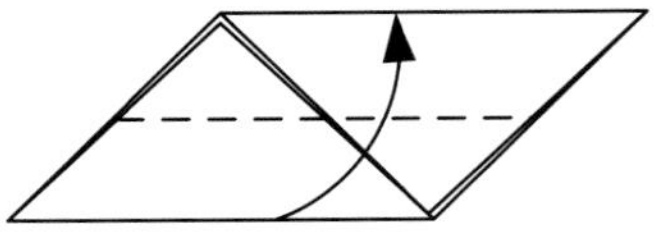

6

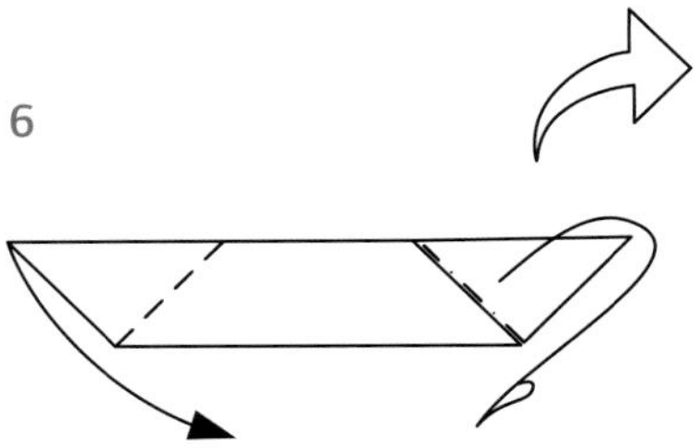

7

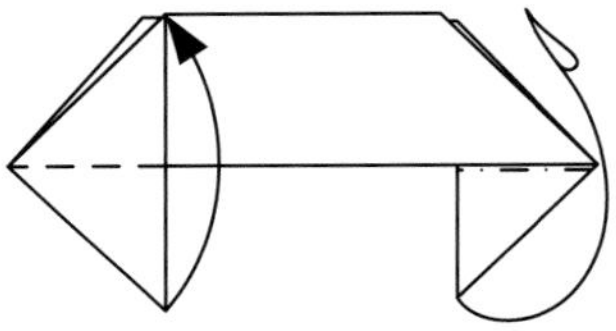

8

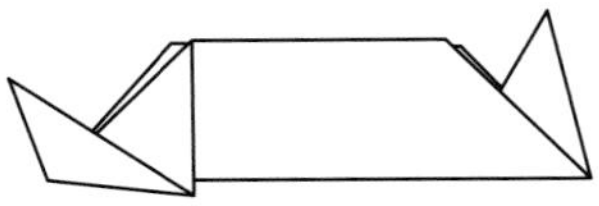

9

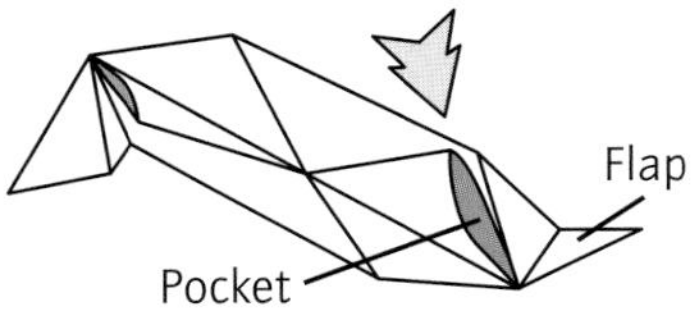

Flap

Pocket

Top view: push on the tiny
flaps to open them

Farandola Florida ✳

PAPER: 6–10 cm (2 ¼–4 inches) square

NUMBER OF UNITS: 30

This is a ball with big petals that can be open or curled. Duo paper works best for this model.

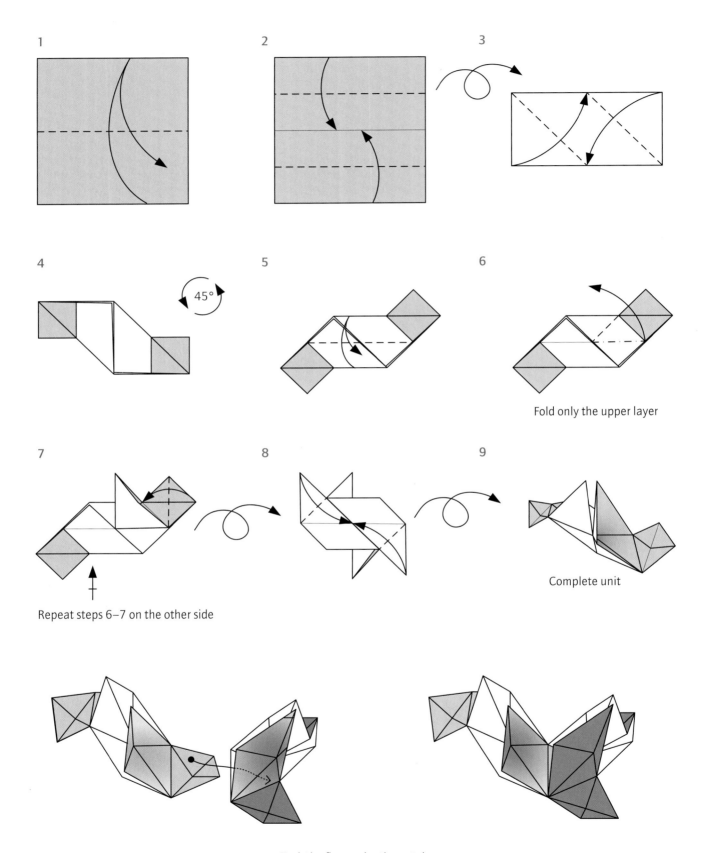

1

2

3

4

45°

5

6

Fold only the upper layer

7

Repeat steps 6–7 on the other side

8

9

Complete unit

Tuck the flap under the petal
Use the assembly method on page 4

VARIATION

Work steps 1-5 of the Farandola Florida, then change it to the following:

6

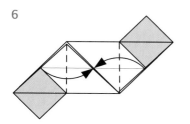

Start with step 6 on page 8

6a

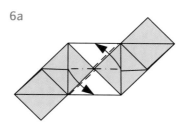

Continue other steps on page 8

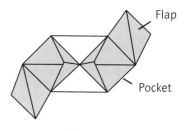

Flap

Pocket

Complete unit

Continue with steps 7–9 of the diagram
Use the assembly method on page 4

VARIATION WITH CURLS

Take the complete Farandola Florida unit and curl the petals instead of opening them. Use the assembly method on page 4.

Farandola Granda ✳✳✳

PAPER: **6–10 cm (2 ¼–4 inches) square**

NUMBER OF UNITS: **30**

This ball has gorgeous flowers. Duo paper works best for this model. The connection method may seem tricky, but once you've connected the last units the result is well worth your efforts!

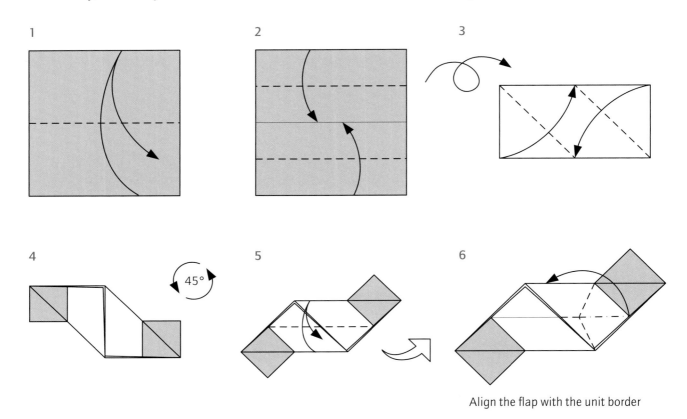

Align the flap with the unit border

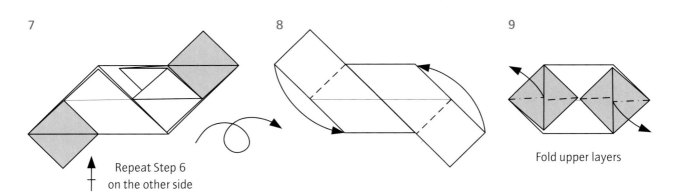

Repeat Step 6 on the other side

Fold upper layers

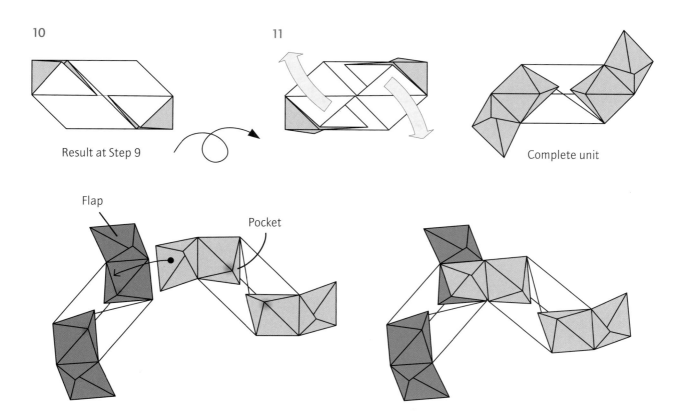

10

Result at Step 9

11

Complete unit

Flap

Pocket

Tuck the flap into the tiny pocket underneath the petal, using tweezers if needed

Use the assembly method on page 4

IF YOU WANT MORE

This is a simplified version of Farandola Granda: fold flap on step 6 of the previous diagram as shown. Follow the remaining steps of the Farandola Granda diagram.

6

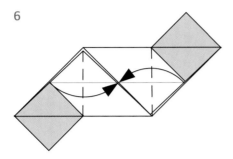

Use the assembly method on page 4

Whirlpool *

PAPER: rectangular with proportions 2:3. See page xiv for how to cut this rectangle from a square. I'd recommend papers of 5 x 7.5 cm (2 x 2¾ inches) or larger.

NUMBER OF UNITS: 30

The petals create the illusion of whirlpools.

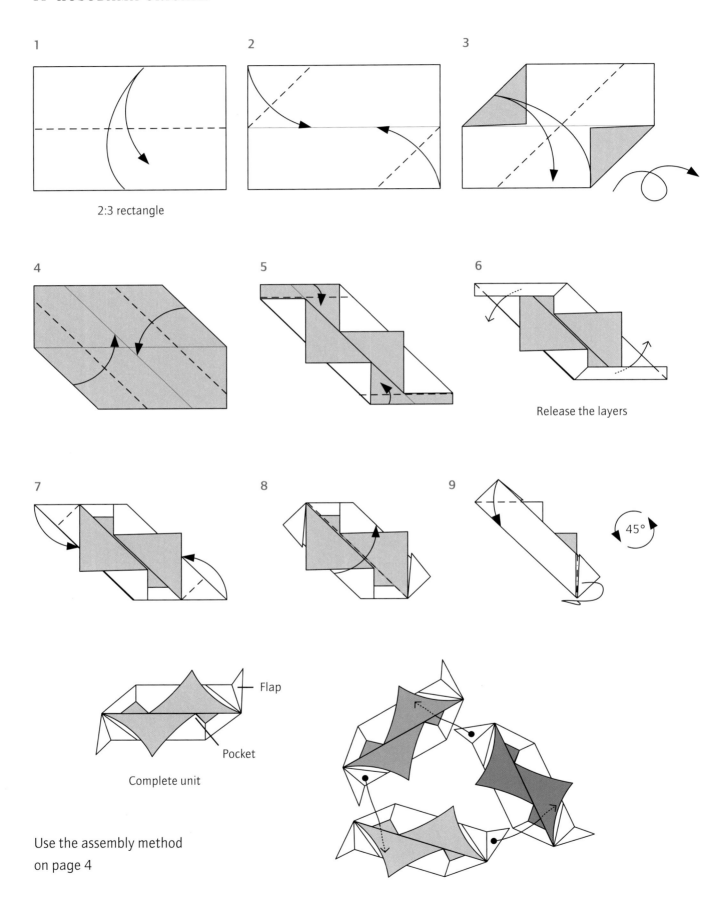

1

2:3 rectangle

2

3

4

5

6

Release the layers

7

8

9

45°

Flap

Pocket

Complete unit

Use the assembly method
on page 4

Spaceship ✳✳

PAPER: 6–10 cm (2¼–4 inches) square

NUMBER OF UNITS: 6,12, or 30

This is a very lightweight ball with strict lines and tiny hills. Various colored, patterned or textured paper works best for this model.

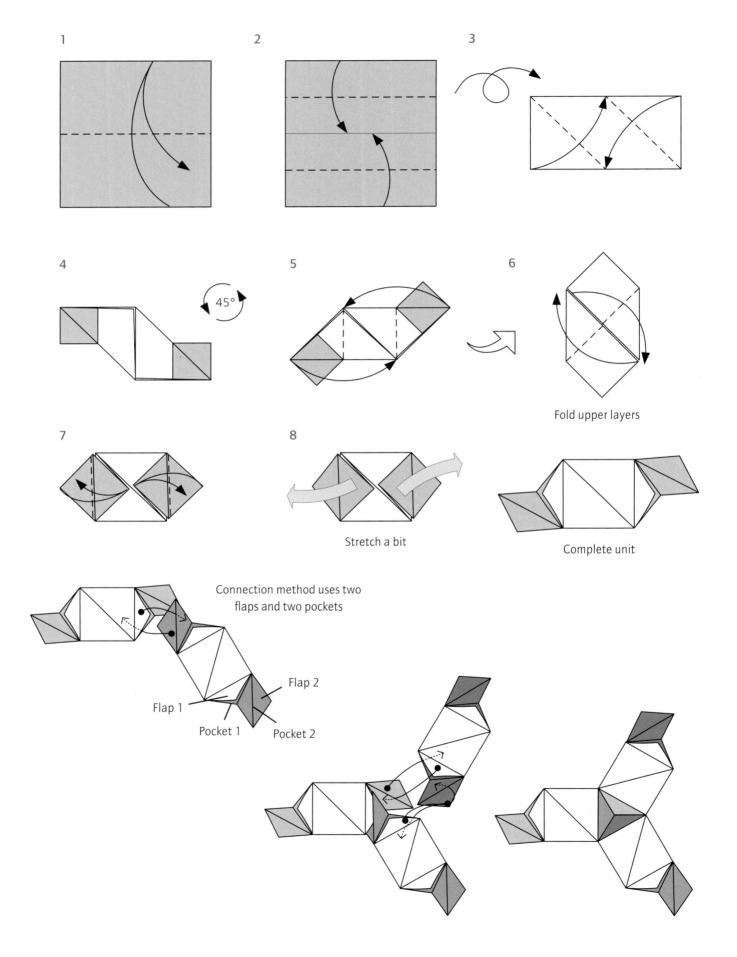

1

2

3

4

45°

5

6

Fold upper layers

7

8

Stretch a bit

Complete unit

Connection method uses two
flaps and two pockets

Flap 1

Flap 2

Pocket 1

Pocket 2

6-UNIT ASSEMBLY (TETRAHEDRON)

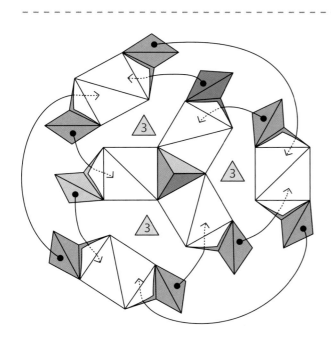

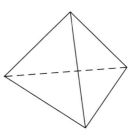

Connect 3 units; then connect other units so that you get a triangular window between the units. Each unit corresponds to the edge of tetrahedron.

12-UNIT ASSEMBLY (CUBE)

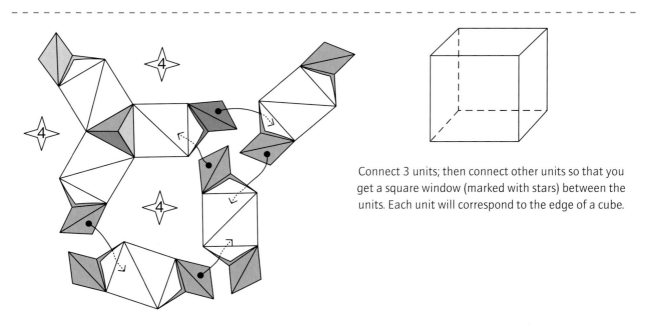

Connect 3 units; then connect other units so that you get a square window (marked with stars) between the units. Each unit will correspond to the edge of a cube.

30-UNIT ASSEMBLY (DODECAHEDRON)

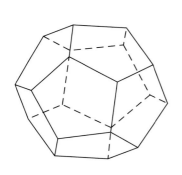

Connect 3 units, then connect other units so that you get a pentangonal window (marked with stars) between the units. Each unit corresponds to the edge of the dodecahedron.

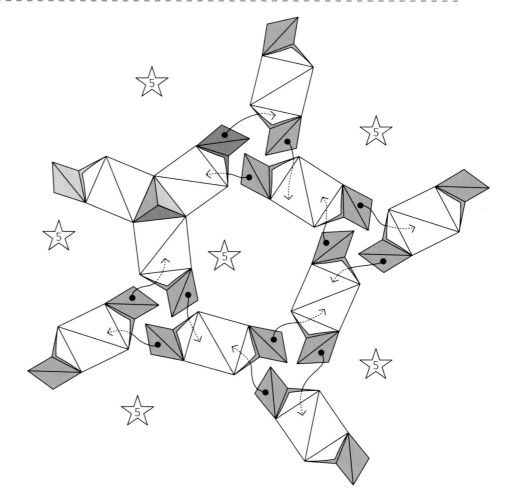

Jade ✳✳

PAPER: 6–10 cm (2¼–4 inches) square

NUMBER OF UNITS: 12 or 30

This is an elegant and easy model with very strong connectors. Try it and you will definitely like it!
Use different colored squares and you will get interesting tracery.

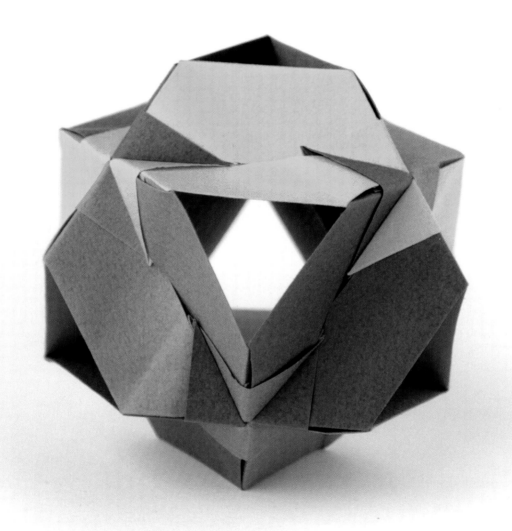

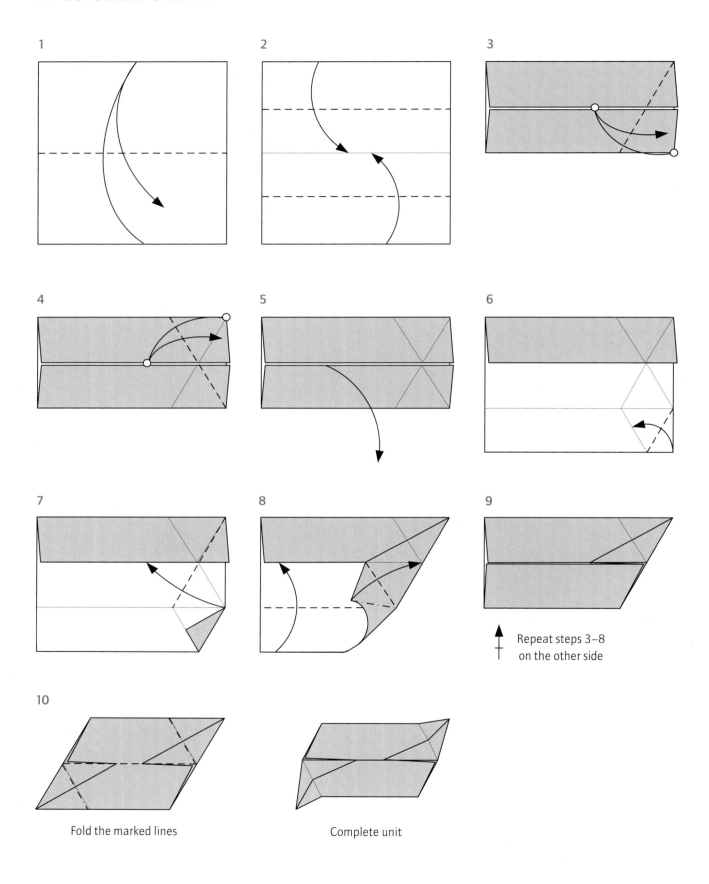

Fold the marked lines

Complete unit

To connect units, tuck a big flap into a big pocket and a small flap in a small pocket at the same time

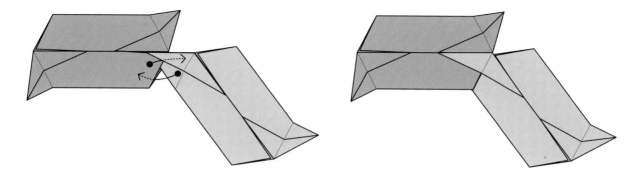

12-UNIT ASSEMBLY: use the assembly method on page 3

30-UNIT ASSEMBLY: use the assembly method on page 4

Sparkling Jade ✳✳

PAPER: 6–10 cm (2¼–4 inches) square

NUMBER OF UNITS: 12 or 30

This is an elegant and easy model with very strong connectors. Duo paper works best for this model: you get pretty sparkles.
Start from step 5 of the Jade diagram.

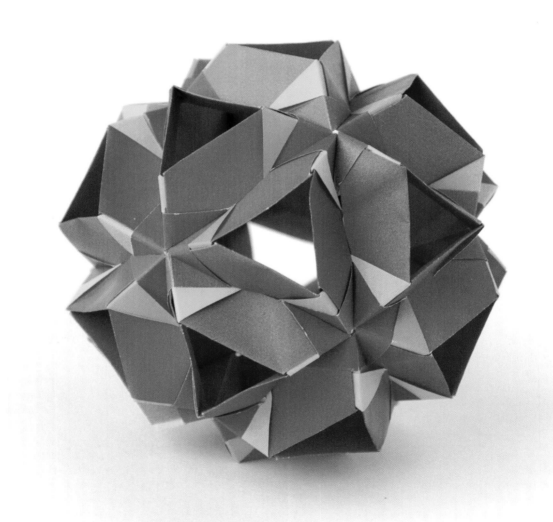

5

6

7

8

9

10

11

12

Repeat steps 3–8 on the other side

Fold the marked lines

Complete unit

Connect units the same way you connect Jade units (see page with Jade)

12-UNIT ASSEMBLY: use the assembly method on page 3

30-UNIT ASSEMBLY: use the assembly method on page 4

Shining Jade ✳✳✳

PAPER: **6–10 cm (2¼–4 inches) square**

NUMBER OF UNITS: **30**

Use duo paper for this variation and shining stars will appear.
Start with step 10 of the Jade diagram (see page 20).

10

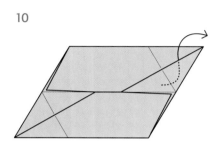

Release the paper

11

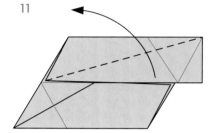

12

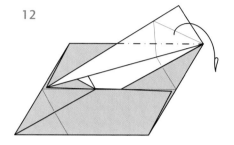

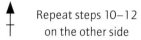

Repeat steps 10–12
on the other side

13

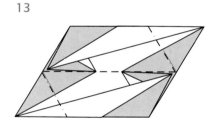

Fold the marked lines

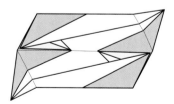

Complete unit

Connect units the same way as
Jade units (see page 21). Use the
assembly method on page 4.

Gem ✳✳✳✳

PAPER: 8–12 cm (3⅛–4¾ inches) square

NUMBER OF UNITS: 30

If you use duo paper, sparkles will appear from the inside of the model.
Start with the complete Sparkling Jade unit.

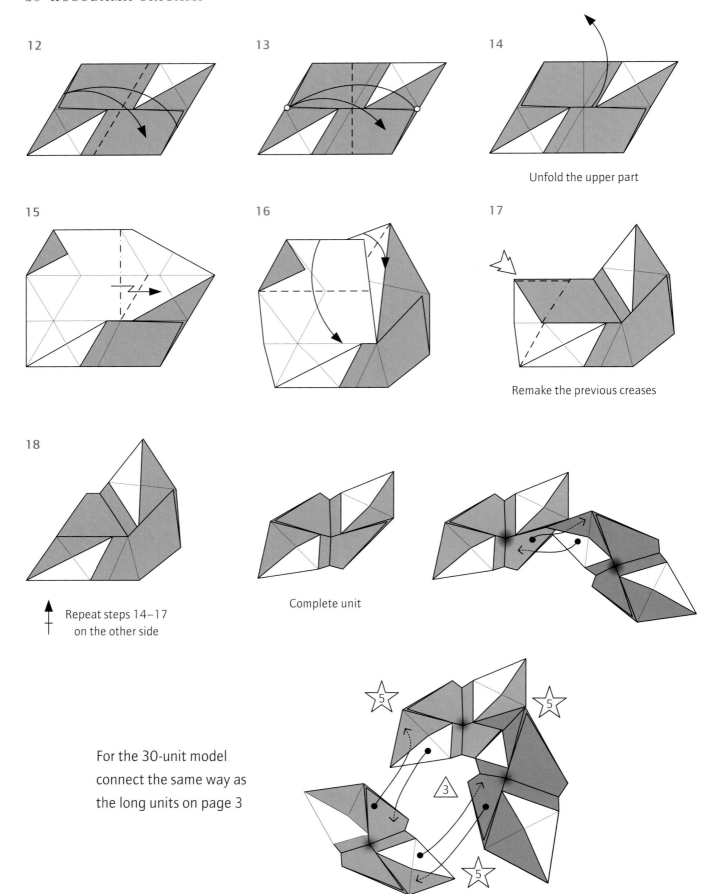

12

13

14

Unfold the upper part

15

16

17

Remake the previous creases

18

Repeat steps 14–17
on the other side

Complete unit

For the 30-unit model
connect the same way as
the long units on page 3

Airy Jade ✳✳

PAPER: rectangular (you can use any proportion, but all the units must be the same size)

NUMBER OF UNITS: 12 or 30

Use long rectangles and get a very airy model. The picture given is for a 1:2 rectangle, but that's not a must. The main idea is that you follow the same steps as in the Jade unit with a rectangle of any size.

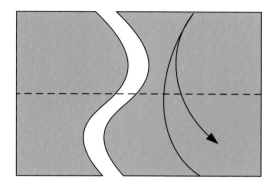

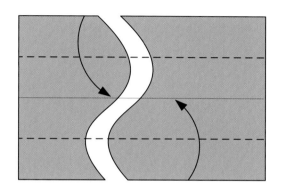

Take rectangle of any proportion
1 : X, where X > 2/√3

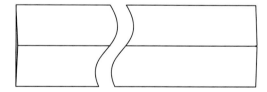

Follow steps 3–8 of the Jade
diagram for both sides

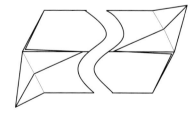

See page 4 for reference on
assembly of a 30-unit model

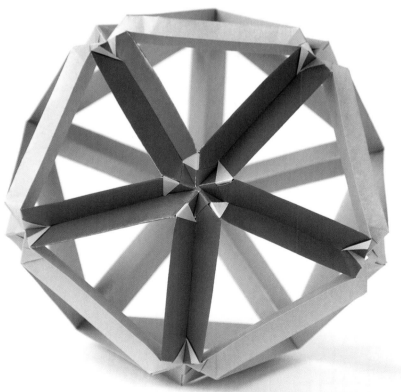

Hypnose ✳✳

PAPER: 6–10 cm (2¼–4 inches) square

NUMBER OF UNITS: 12 or 30

This model has tiny curls.

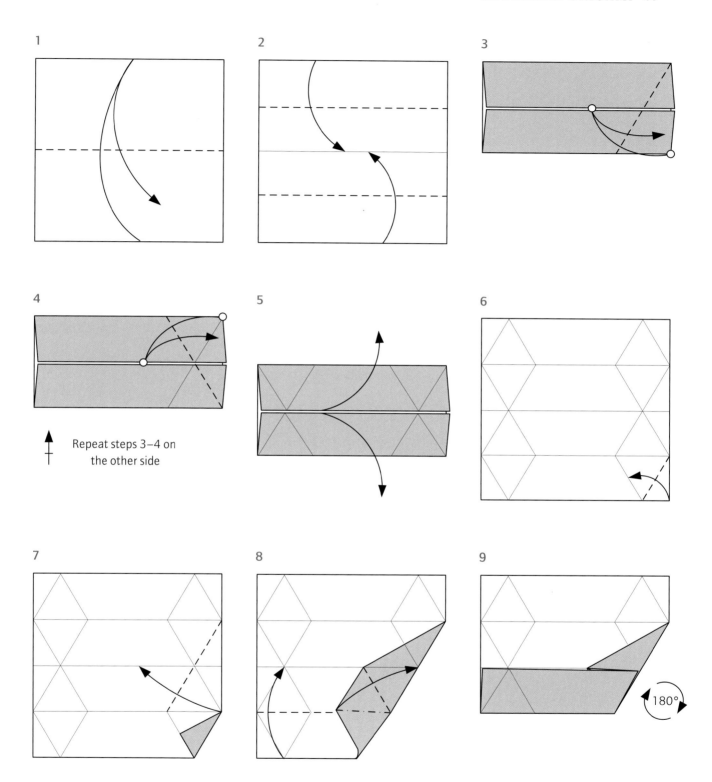

1

2

3

4

Repeat steps 3–4 on the other side

5

6

7

8

9

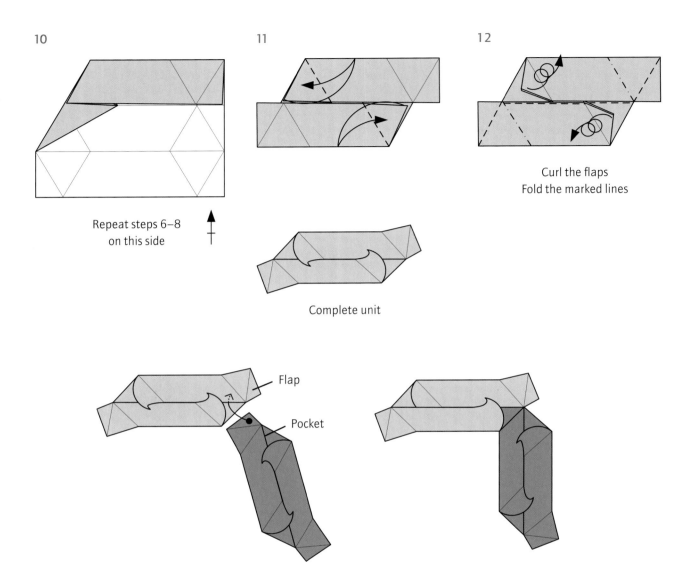

10

Repeat steps 6–8
on this side

11

Complete unit

12

Curl the flaps
Fold the marked lines

Flap

Pocket

12-UNIT ASSEMBLY: use the assembly method on page 3

30-UNIT ASSEMBLY: use the assembly method on page 4

Coquette **

PAPER: **6–10 cm (2¼–4 inches) square**

NUMBER OF UNITS: **12 or 30**

This model has tiny petals. Use duo paper to get petals that contrast in color with the whole model.

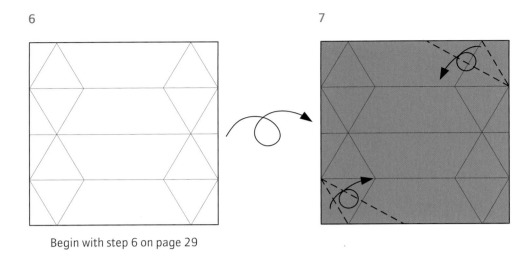

6

7

Begin with step 6 on page 29

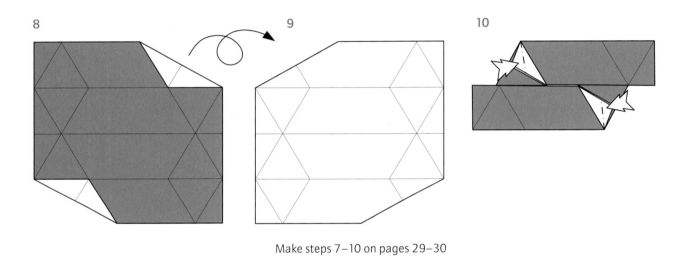

8

9

10

Make steps 7–10 on pages 29–30

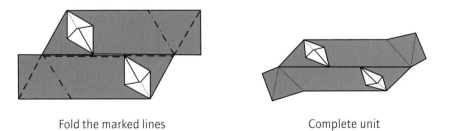

Fold the marked lines

Complete unit

Connect using the same steps as the Hypnose unit (page 28).

12-UNIT ASSEMBLY: use the assembly method on page 3

30-UNIT ASSEMBLY: use the assembly method on page 4

CHAPTER 2

Sparaxis Flower **

PAPER: **6 -10 cm (2 ¼–4 inches) square**

NUMBER OF UNITS: **5-8**

This flower is fast and easy to make. You can use it for various handmade projects or as an addition to the floral balls.

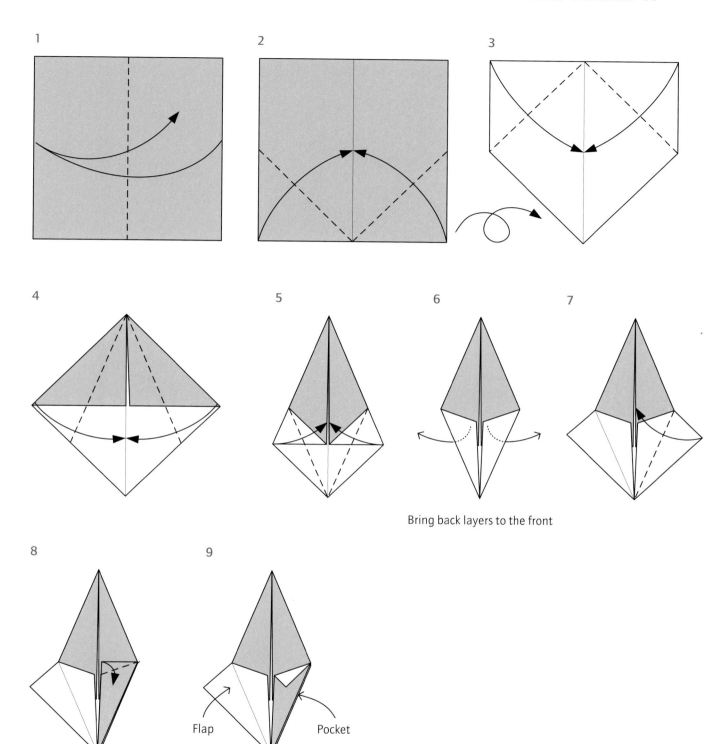

1

2

3

4

5

6

7

Bring back layers to the front

8

9

Flap   Pocket

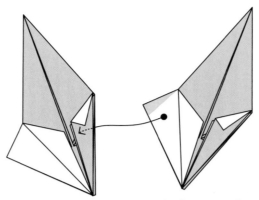

The pocket is slightly smaller than the flap. Open the pocket completely, tuck the flap in and then reclose the pocket. The dark part of the flap becomes locked. Units hold together very tightly.

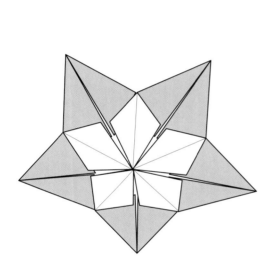

5 unit assembly: the 3-D flower

8 unit assembly: the flat star

Sparaxis ✳ ✳ ✳

PAPER: Use a rectangle with a 1:2 proportion. See page xii for how to cut this rectangle from a square. Use paper sized 5 x 10 cm (2 x 4 inches) or larger.

NUMBER OF UNITS: 18 or 30

This model has delightful flowers that appear to blossom out from the center. Each flower has two rows of petals.

30-unit model, see page 41

18-unit model, see page 40

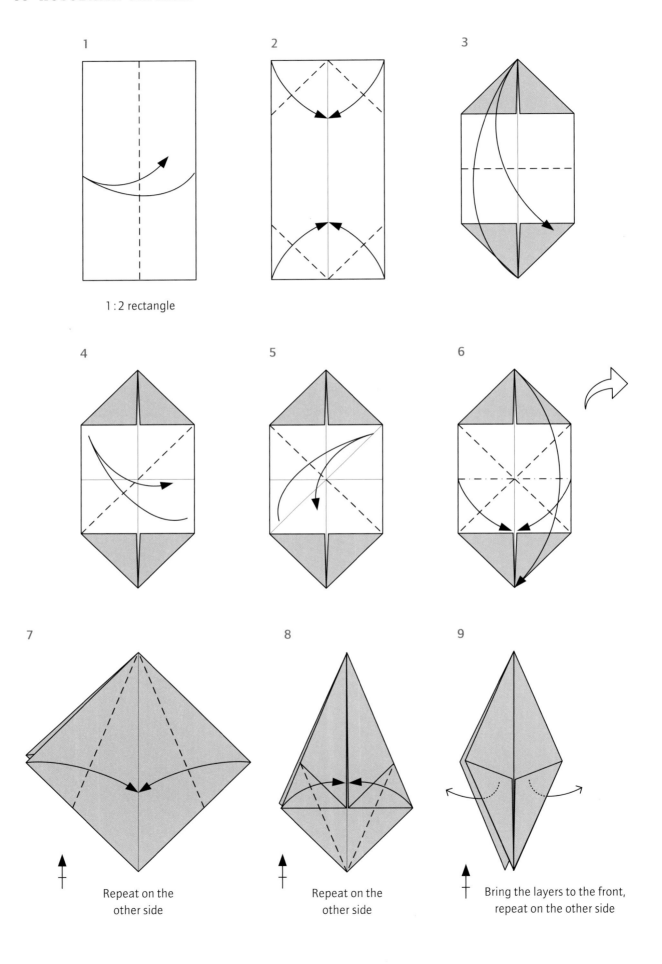

1:2 rectangle

Repeat on the
other side

Repeat on the
other side

Bring the layers to the front,
repeat on the other side

10 **11**

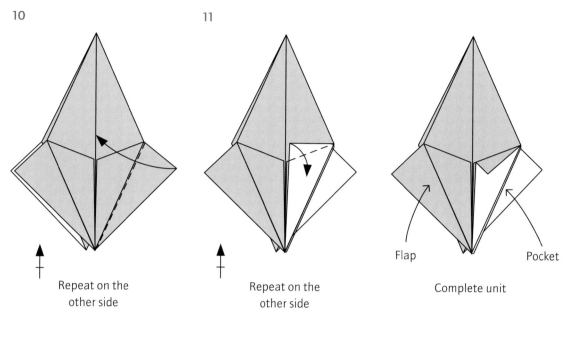

Repeat on the
other side

Repeat on the
other side

Flap

Pocket

Complete unit

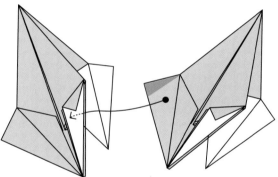

The pocket is slightly smaller than the flap. Open the pocket
completely, tuck the flap in and then reclose the pocket. The dark
part of the flap becomes locked. Units hold together very tightly.

18-UNIT ASSEMBLY

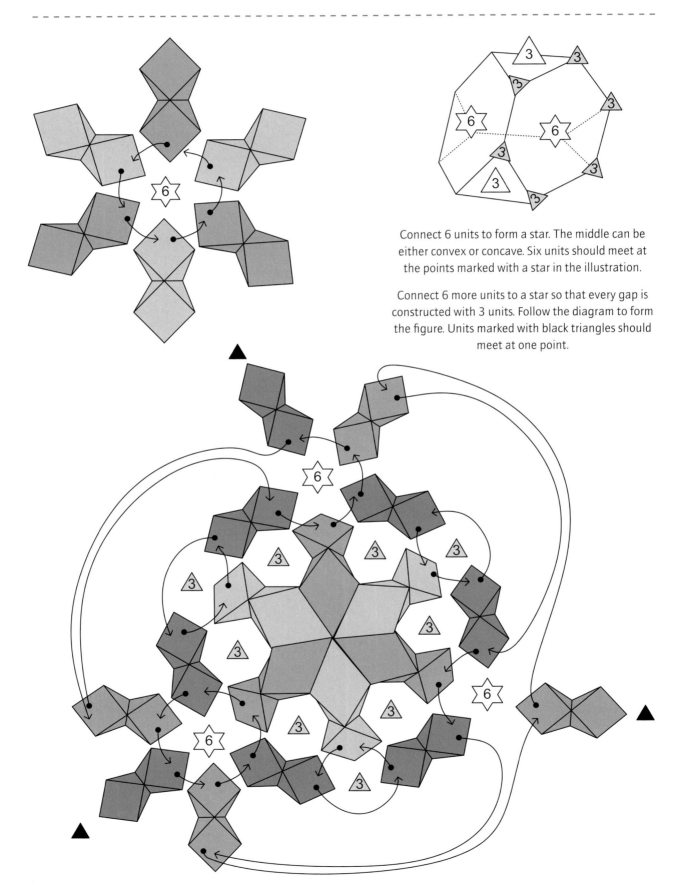

Connect 6 units to form a star. The middle can be either convex or concave. Six units should meet at the points marked with a star in the illustration.

Connect 6 more units to a star so that every gap is constructed with 3 units. Follow the diagram to form the figure. Units marked with black triangles should meet at one point.

30-UNIT ASSEMBLY

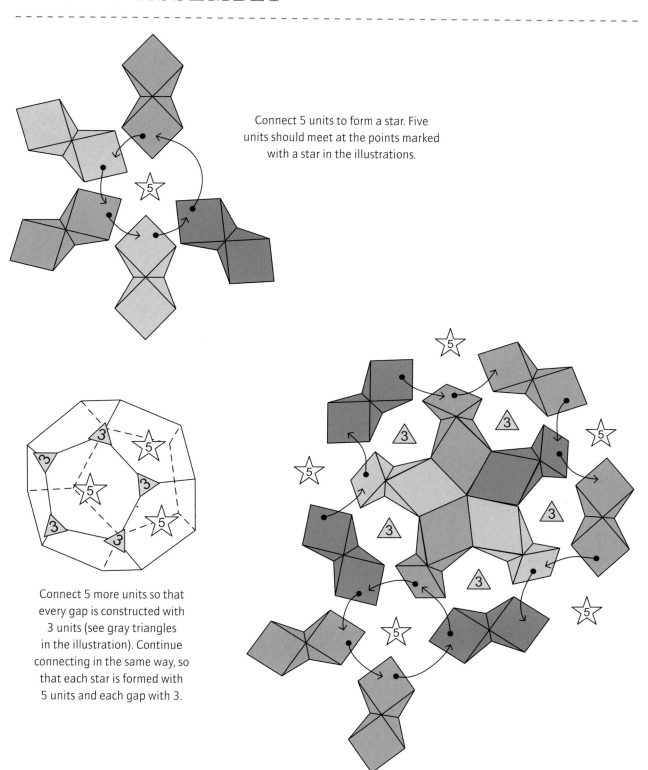

Connect 5 units to form a star. Five units should meet at the points marked with a star in the illustrations.

Connect 5 more units so that every gap is constructed with 3 units (see gray triangles in the illustration). Continue connecting in the same way, so that each star is formed with 5 units and each gap with 3.

Bitterroot ✳ ✳ ✳

PAPER: Use a rectangle with a 1:2 proportion. See page xii for how to cut this rectangle from a square. Use paper sized 5 x 10 cm (2 x 4 inches) or larger.

NUMBER OF UNITS: 5, 6, or 7 for a star; 12, 18, or 30 for a floral ball.

This model has hills, covered with petals and spikes. Depending upon the paper you use, you can make the main airy version or the solid variation.

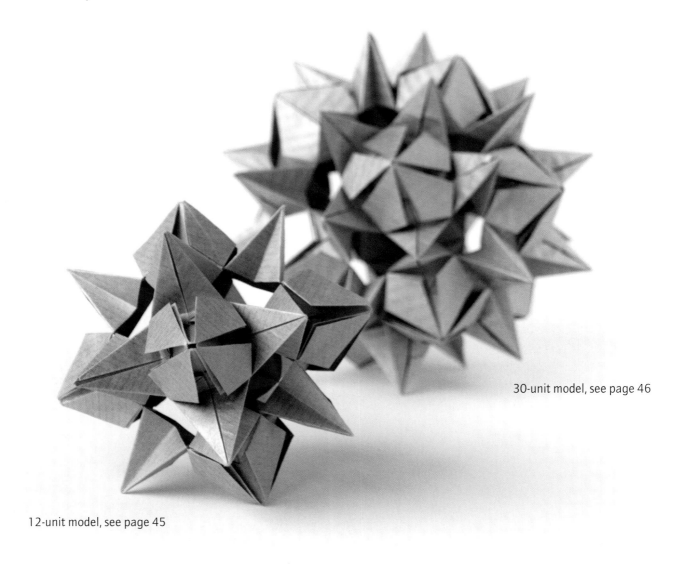

30-unit model, see page 46

12-unit model, see page 45

1

2

3

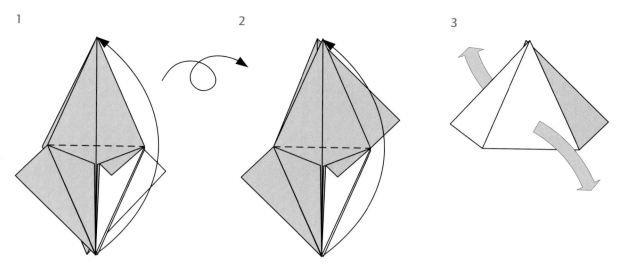

Take the complete Sparaxis unit

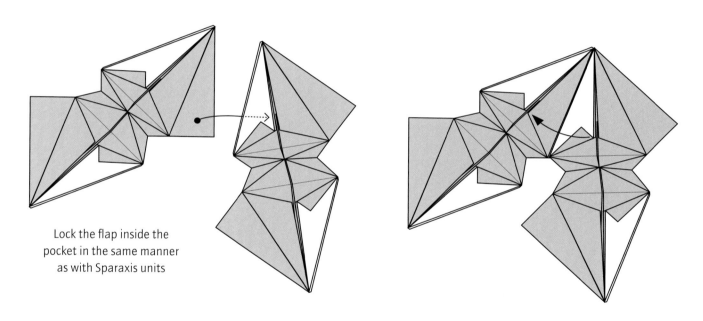

Lock the flap inside the
pocket in the same manner
as with Sparaxis units

ASSEMBLY TO A STAR

This is a simple way to get good results with minimal effort, particularly if you are a novice to modular origami. These stars would make perfect New Year's decorations.

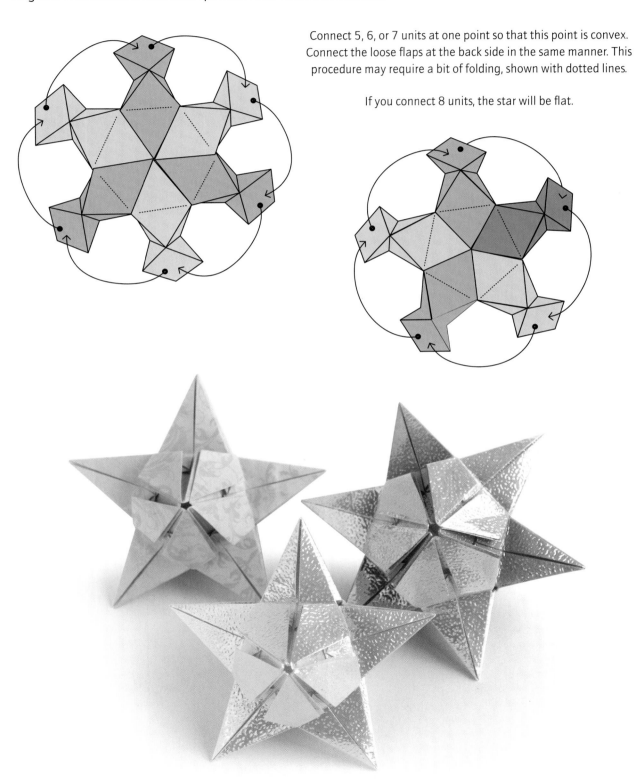

Connect 5, 6, or 7 units at one point so that this point is convex. Connect the loose flaps at the back side in the same manner. This procedure may require a bit of folding, shown with dotted lines.

If you connect 8 units, the star will be flat.

12-UNIT ASSEMBLY

Unlike Sparaxis units, the Bitterroot model can also be assembled with 12 units.

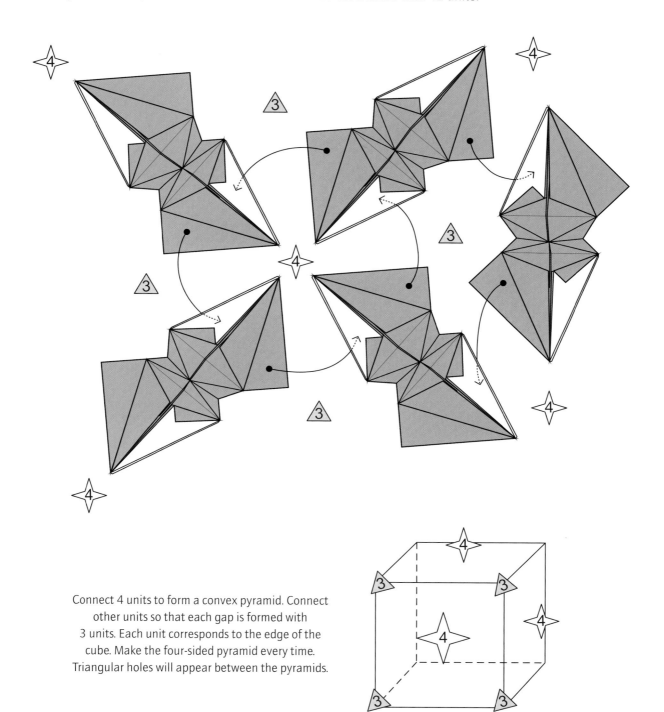

Connect 4 units to form a convex pyramid. Connect other units so that each gap is formed with 3 units. Each unit corresponds to the edge of the cube. Make the four-sided pyramid every time. Triangular holes will appear between the pyramids.

30-UNIT ASSEMBLY

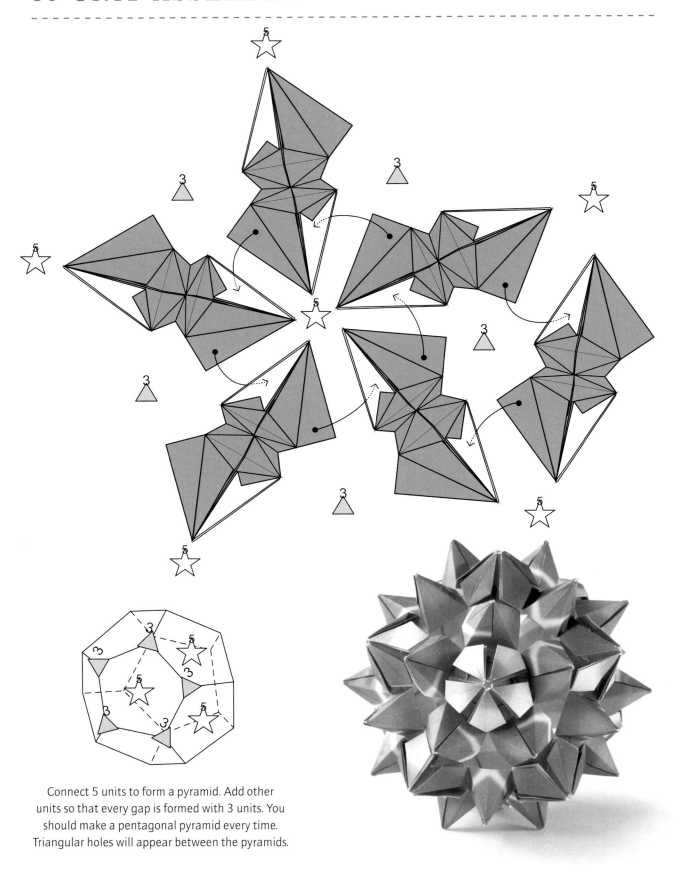

Connect 5 units to form a pyramid. Add other units so that every gap is formed with 3 units. You should make a pentagonal pyramid every time. Triangular holes will appear between the pyramids.

Bitterroot Variation ✳✳✳

PAPER: Use a rectangle with a 1:2 proportion. See page xii for how to cut this rectangle from a square. Use paper sized 5 x 10 cm (2 x 4 inches) or larger.

NUMBER OF UNITS: 12, 18, or 30

Use the completed Bitterroot unit. Hide the loose paper inside the unit.
Use the assembly methods on pages 45 and 46. The methods on pages 40 and 41 can also be used.

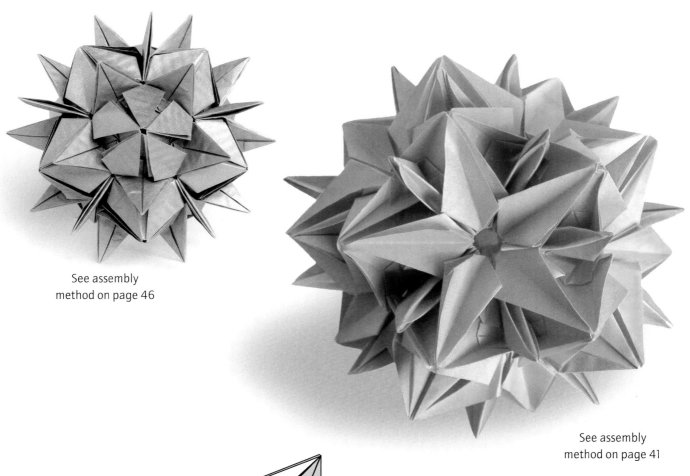

See assembly
method on page 46

See assembly
method on page 41

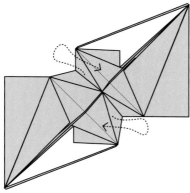
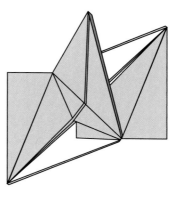

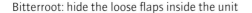
Bitterroot: hide the loose flaps inside the unit

Mandragora ✳✳✳

PAPER: Use a rectangle with a 1:2 proportion. See page xii for how to cut this rectangle from a square. Use paper sized 6 x 12 cm (2k¼ x 4 inches) or larger.

NUMBER OF UNITS: 18 or 30

This flower ball has very delicate flowers. Inset different colored pieces of paper to make the flowers even more interesting. You can achieve a good effect even if you have plain papers. Play with color combinations and you'll see how different this model can look.

Start with the Sparaxis unit on page 38. You can use the same connection diagrams as for the Sparaxis unit on pages 40 and 41.

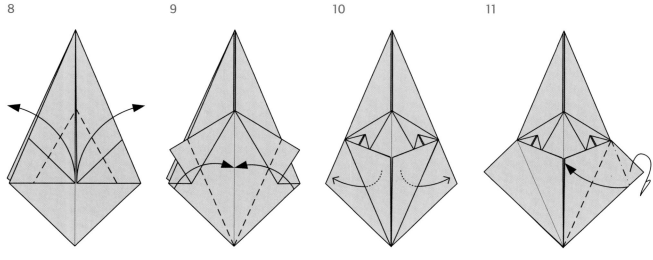

8 9 10 11

Make the unit using the diagram on page 38 until you reach step 8, then continue as shown above

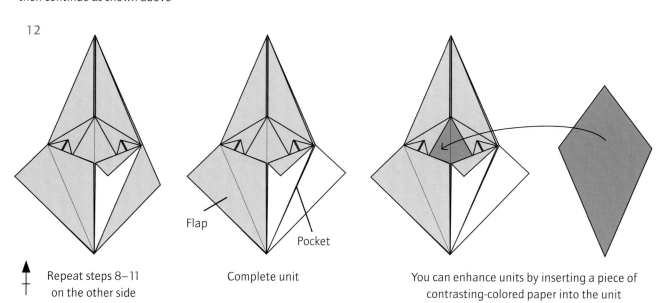

12

Repeat steps 8–11 on the other side

Flap

Pocket

Complete unit

You can enhance units by inserting a piece of contrasting-colored paper into the unit

18-unit model, see page 40
for assembly method

30-unit model, see page 41
for assembly method

Crocus ✳✳✳

PAPER: Use a rectangle with 1:2 proportions. See page xii for how to cut this rectangle from a square. Use paper sized 5 x 10 cm (2 x 4 inches) or larger.

NUMBER OF UNITS: 18 or 30

With its austere symbolic flowers, this model is somewhere between naturalism and geometry. Various-colored or patterned papers will work well for this ball.

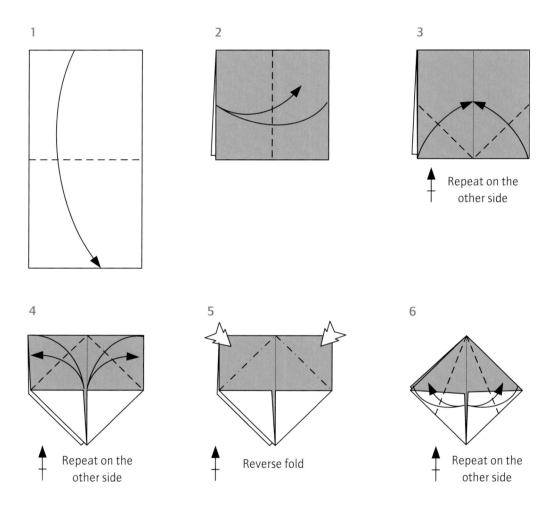

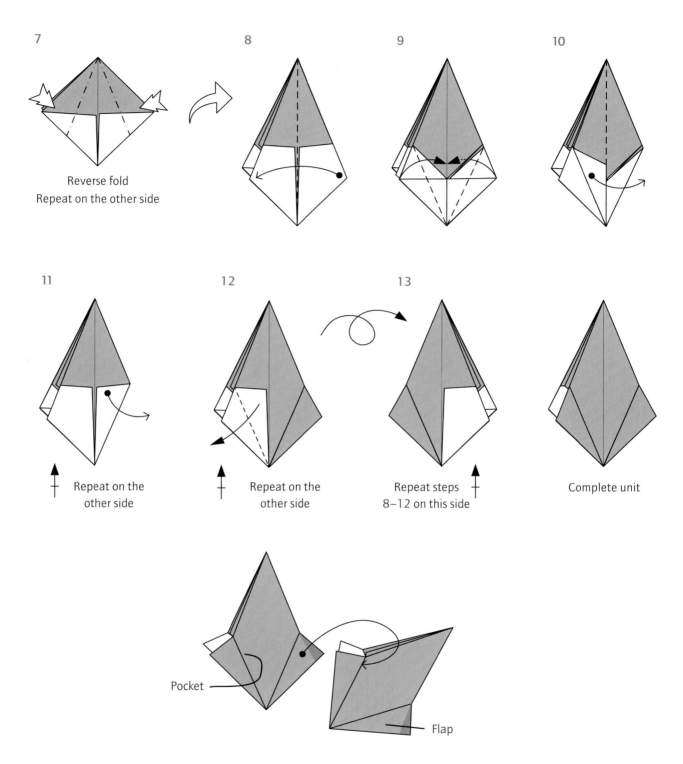

7

Reverse fold
Repeat on the other side

8

9

10

11

Repeat on the
other side

12

Repeat on the
other side

13

Repeat steps
8–12 on this side

Complete unit

Pocket

Flap

Open the pocket completely, tuck the flap in, close the pocket. The flap
becomes locked by the pocket. Petals will hold together because the triangle
marked in the illustration above is locked by the crease of the pocket.

18-unit model, see page 40
for assembly method

30-unit model, see page 41
for assembly method

You can also use the same assembly methods as for the Sparaxis unit.

Dollar Crocus ✳✳✳

PAPER: Use a U.S. banknote or a rectangle with the same proportions (see page xiv). You can also use rectangles that are a bit longer or a bit shorter. The only restriction is that all units should be the same size.

NUMBER OF UNITS: 18 or 30

This Crocus model variation is designed specifically for folding dollar bills. It can be used as a monetary gift. Since no glue is used, one can always disassemble the present to use the cash. You don't even need the receipt to cash it!

1

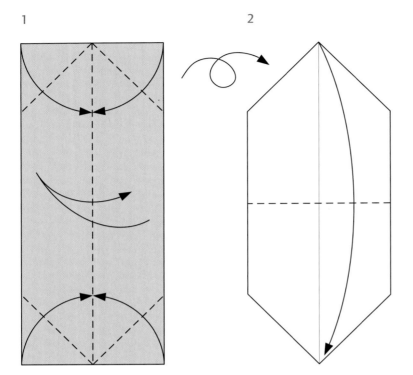

Take 1 U.S. dollar (or maybe more)
Rectangles with a proportion of 1:2.3 (see
page xiv) or near that are also suitable

2

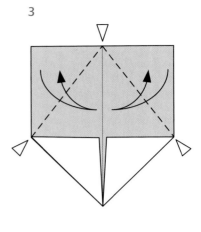

3

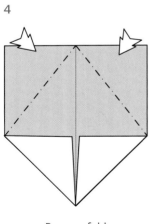

4

Reverse fold

5

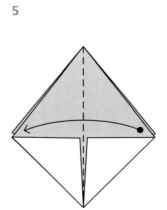

6

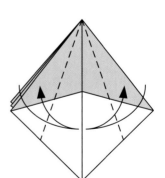

7

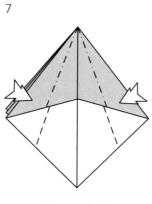

Reverse fold

8

9

10

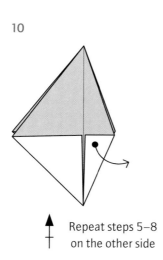

↑ Repeat steps 5–8
† on the other side

Complete unit
Connect the same way as the Crocus units

Use the same connection diagrams as for the Sparaxis unit

18-UNIT ASSEMBLY: use the assembly method on page 40

30-UNIT ASSEMBLY: use the assembly method on page 41

Dollar Sparaxis ✳ ✳ ✳

PAPER: Use a U.S. banknote or a rectangle with the same proportions (see page xiv). You can also use rectangles that are a bit longer or a bit shorter. The only restriction is that all units should be the same size.

NUMBER OF UNITS: 18 or 30

Another valuable gift if you use money for this model: If you use duo paper instead, you will achieve beautiful effects inside the flower.

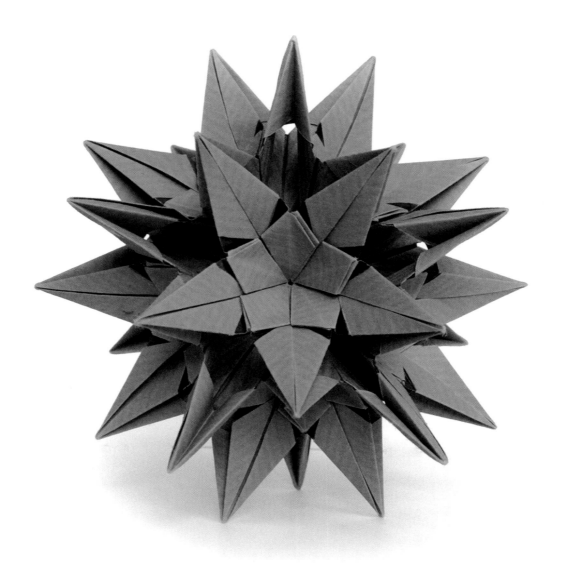

1

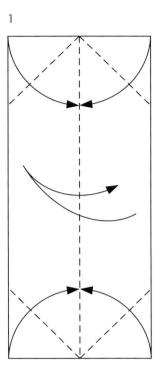

Take 1 U.S. dollar (or maybe more)
Rectangles with a proportion of 1:2.3 (see
page xiv) or near that are also suitable

2

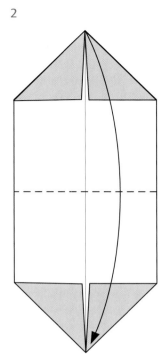

3

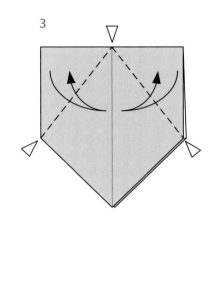

4

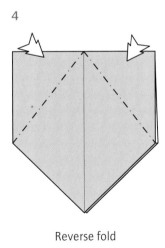

Reverse fold

5

Repeat on
the back side

6

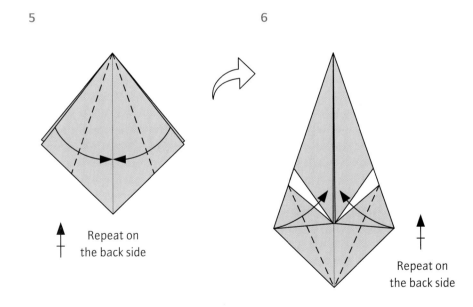

Repeat on
the back side

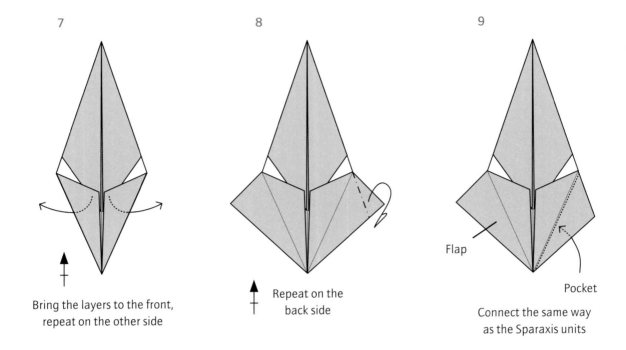

7

Bring the layers to the front,
repeat on the other side

8

Repeat on the
back side

9

Flap

Pocket

Connect the same way
as the Sparaxis units

Use the same connection diagrams as for the Sparaxis unit

18-UNIT ASSEMBLY: **use the assembly method on page 40**

30-UNIT ASSEMBLY: **use the assembly method on page 41**

Arctica ✳✳✳

PAPER: Use a rectangle with 1:3 proportions. See page xiii for how to cut this rectangle from a square. I recommend using rectangles 5 x 15 cm (1¾ x 5⅞ inches) or larger.

NUMBER OF UNITS: 30

This model has super spiky flowers. It reminds me of a big snowflake; that's why I called it Arctica. Duo paper will work best for this piece of ice.

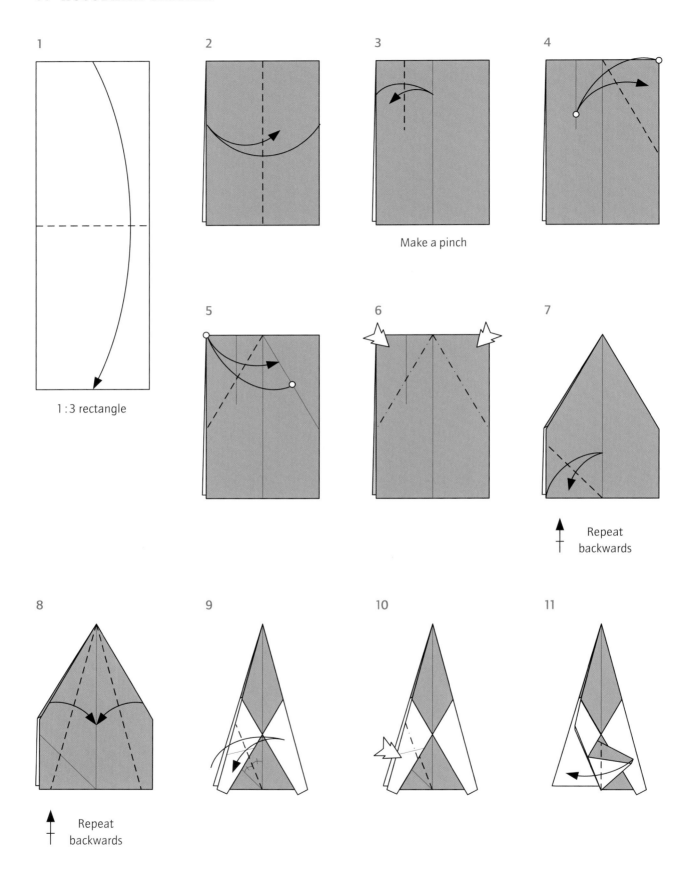

1

1 : 3 rectangle

2

3

Make a pinch

4

5

6

7

Repeat backwards

8

Repeat backwards

9

10

11

12   13   14

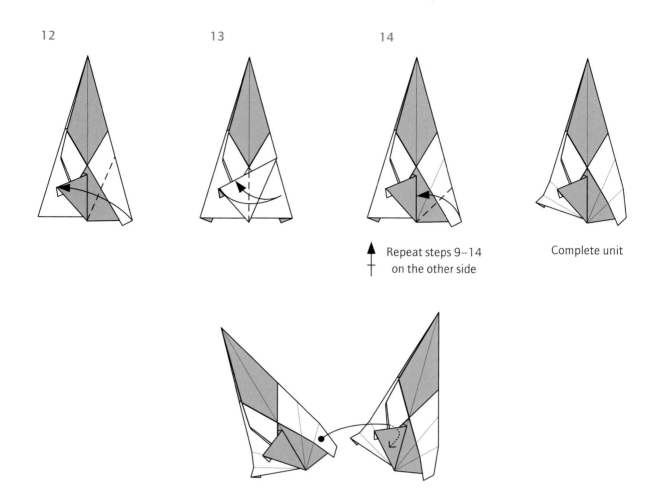

Repeat steps 9–14
on the other side

Complete unit

30-UNIT ASSEMBLY: use the assembly method on page 41

Lilia ✳ ✳ ✳ ✳

- -

PAPER: Use an "A" rectangle. Take A5 paper (half the size of standard printer paper) if you are a novice to modular origami. One quarter of a piece of printer paper will also work well. See page xii for how to cut this rectangle from a square.

NUMBER OF UNITS: 30

The tiny curls inside these flowers make this model look very interesting. Use "harmony" paper if you want to achieve the effect of a flower. The assembly of this flower ball may require using tweezers to tuck the flaps into the pockets.

1

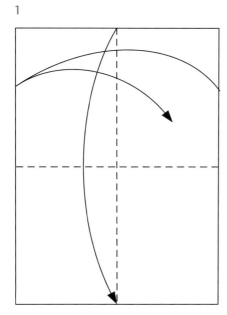

"A" rectangle

2

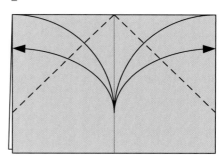

3

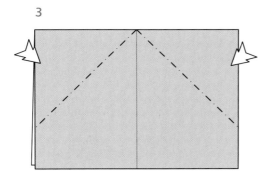

Reverse fold

4

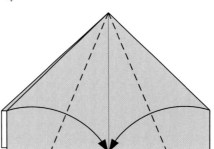

5

6

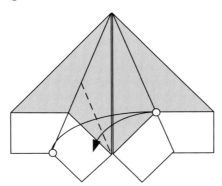

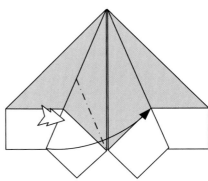

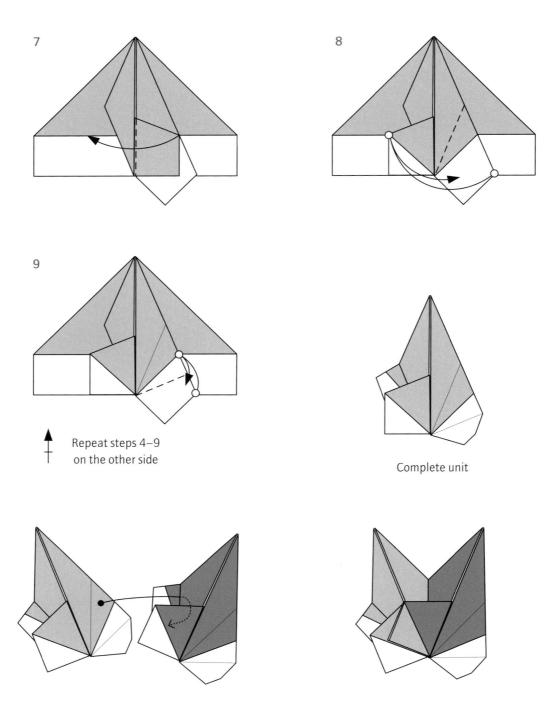

7

8

9

Repeat steps 4–9
on the other side

Complete unit

30-UNIT ASSEMBLY: use the assembly method on page 41

Lilia Star ✳✳

PAPER: Use an "A" rectangle. Take A7 paper (one eighth of a sheet of standard printer paper). See page xii for how to cut this rectangle from a square.

NUMBER OF UNITS: 5-8

Use this star for decoration on postcards or for gift-wrapping. Since an 8-unit star is flat, put it in a letter and your tiny gift can travel thousands of miles. If you assemble less than eight units, you can make the flower with curls, as in the Lilia model.

1

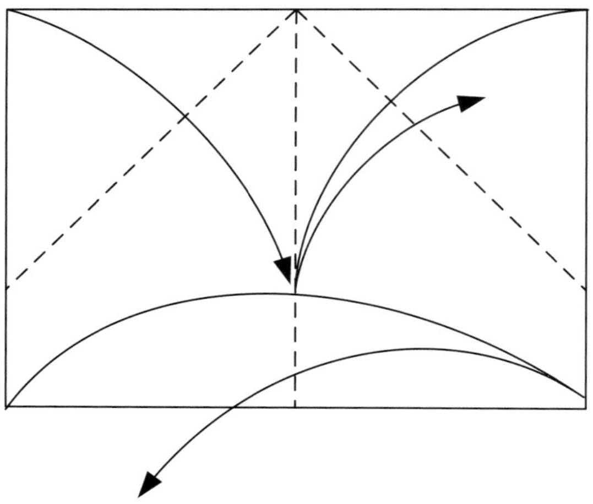

2

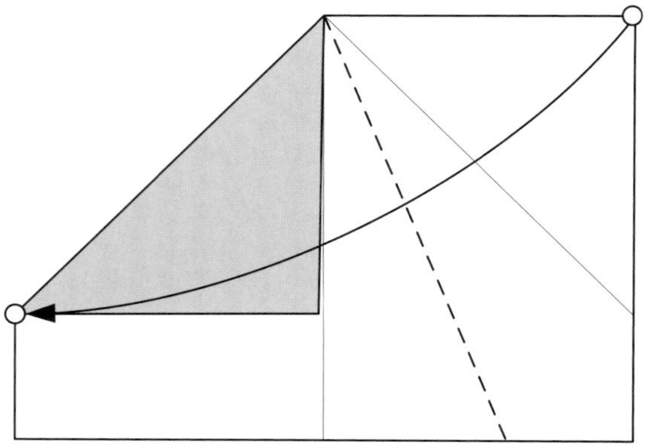

3

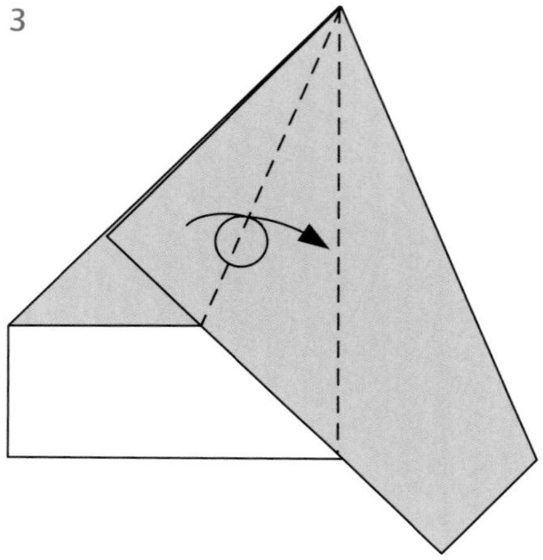

4

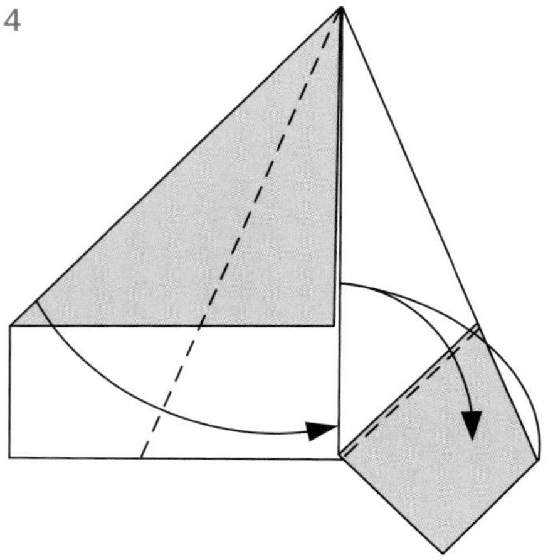

5

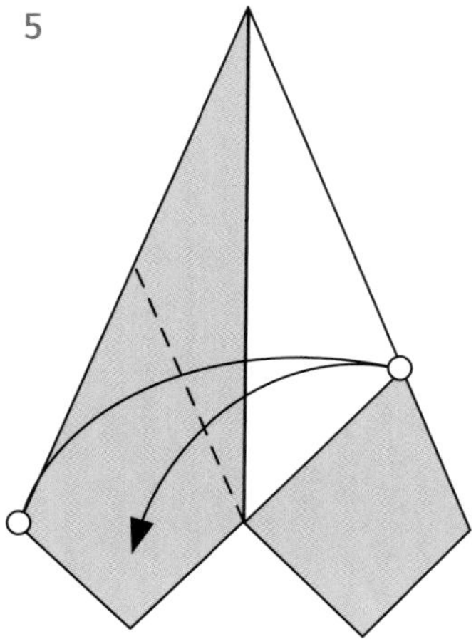

6

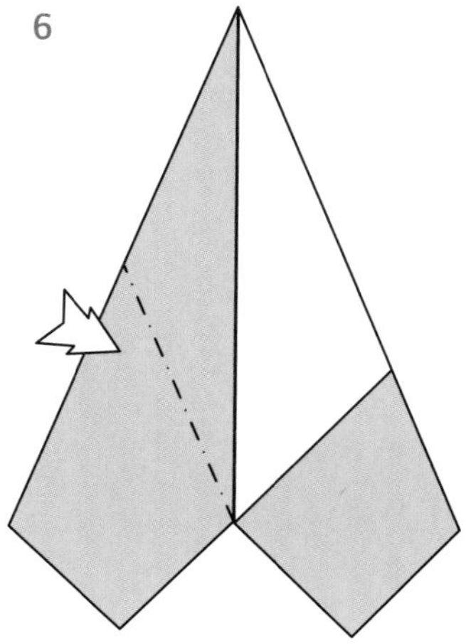

Reverse fold

7

Complete unit

8

Put the flap into the pocket

9

Lock the flap inside by folding. Hide the
edge of the paper in the tiny pocket

+ 5 units

Complete star

LILIA STAR VARIATION

Start with a complete Lilia star unit. Assemble following the steps below.

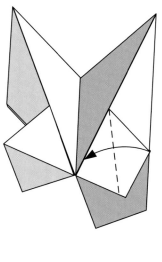 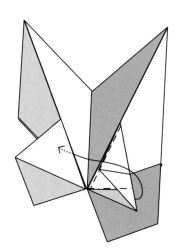 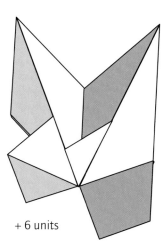

+ 6 units

Complete star

Mandarin ✳✳✳

PAPER: Use a rectangle with 1:2 proportions. See page xii for how to cut this rectangle from a square.
I recommend papers sized 5 x 10 cm (2 x 4 inches) or larger.

NUMBER OF UNITS: 12, 30

Duo paper works best for this model. You get ornamentation on the hills of this ball. Try various color combinations.

1

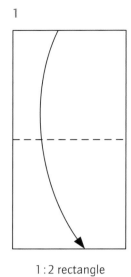

1 : 2 rectangle

2

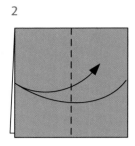

3

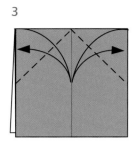

4

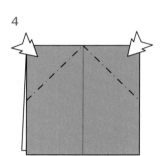

5

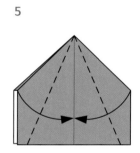

6

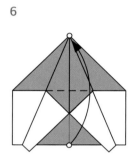

7

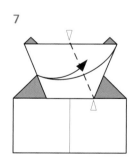

8

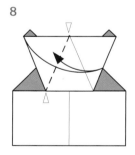

9

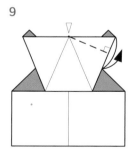

10

11

Reverse fold

12

Release the paper
from underneath

13

Repeat steps 5–13
on the other side

14

Fold the marked lines:
unit is complete

12-UNIT ASSEMBLY: use the assembly method on page 45

30-UNIT ASSEMBLY: use the assembly method on page 46

CHAPTER 3

Alina ✳✳✳✳

PAPER: **Use a 7–10 cm (2 ¾–4 inches) square for each unit**

NUMBER OF UNITS: **12 or 30**

This model has very long petals that seem to grow between the pyramids. It's named after my very good and inspiring friend Alina.

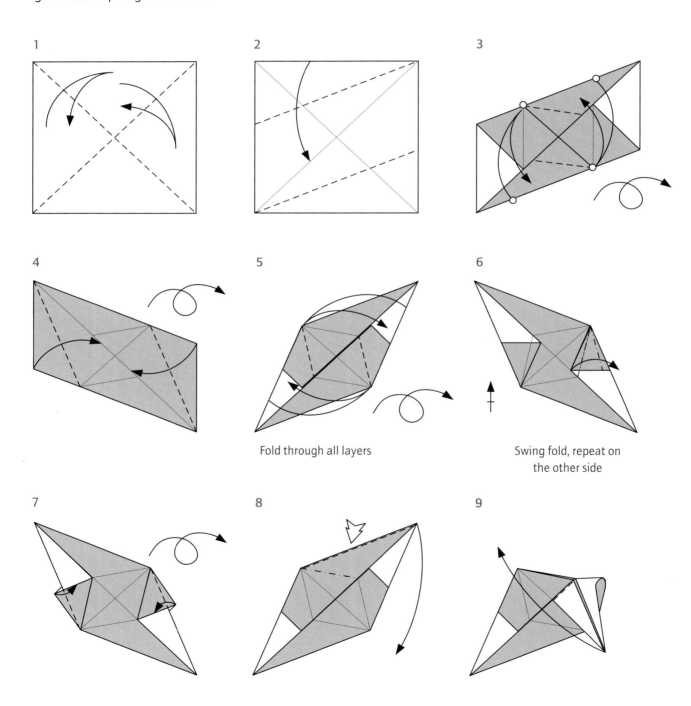

5

Fold through all layers

6

Swing fold, repeat on
the other side

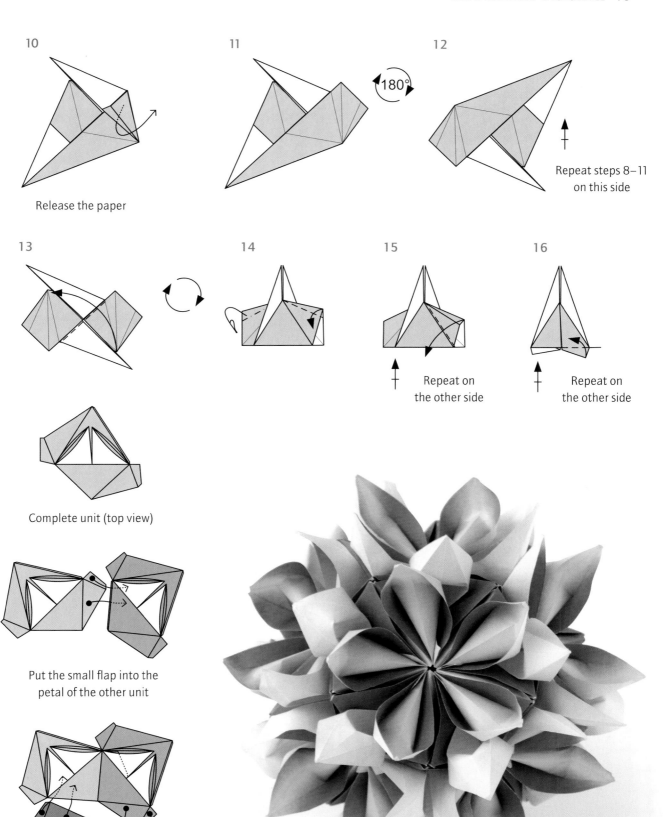

10

Release the paper

11

180°

12

Repeat steps 8–11 on this side

13

14

15

Repeat on the other side

16

Repeat on the other side

Complete unit (top view)

Put the small flap into the petal of the other unit

30-unit assembly with open petals

12-UNIT ASSEMBLY

Each unit is represented symbolically. Each arrow represents the connection method for a particular unit.

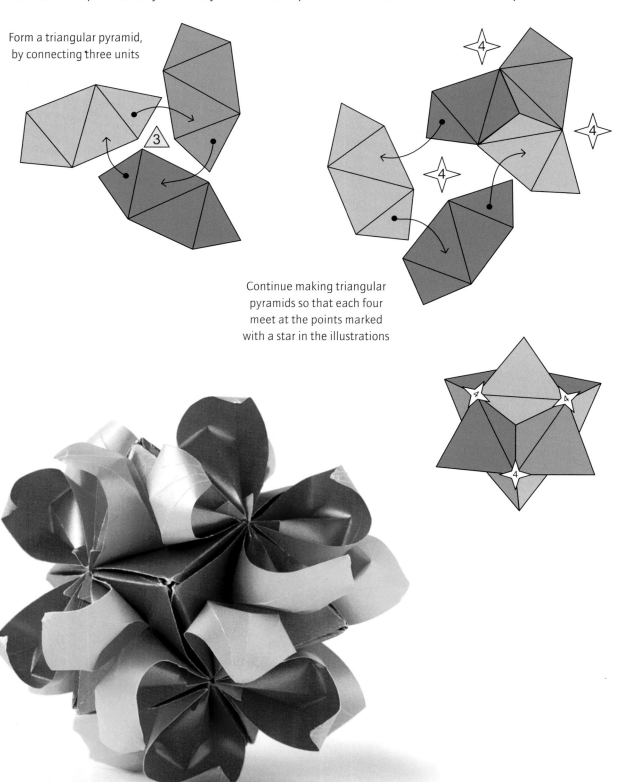

Form a triangular pyramid, by connecting three units

Continue making triangular pyramids so that each four meet at the points marked with a star in the illustrations

30-UNIT ASSEMBLY

Form a triangular pyramid, by connecting three units.

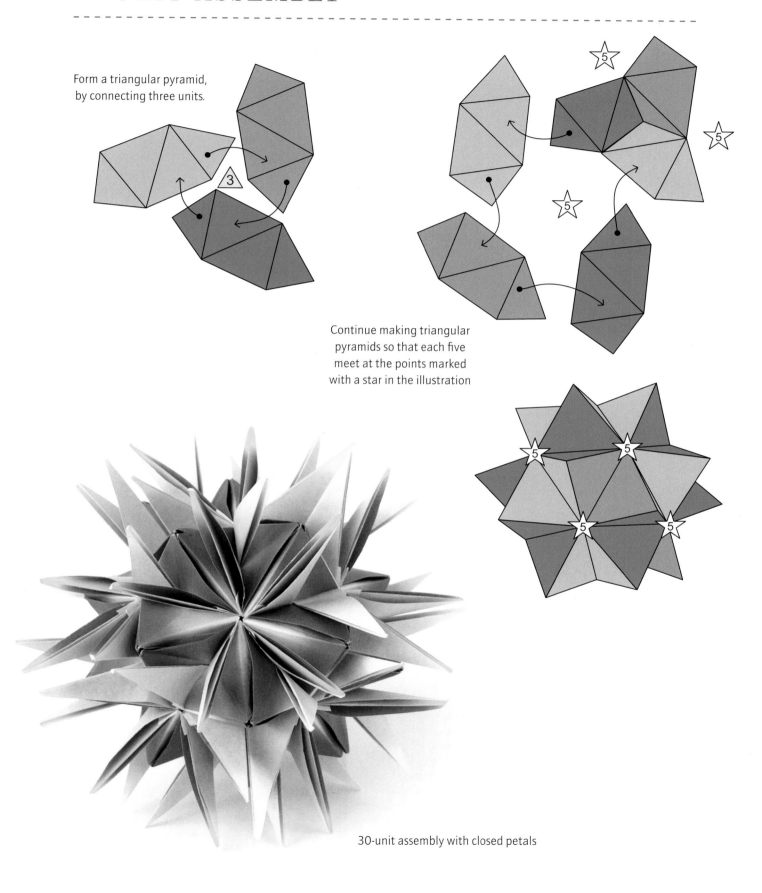

Continue making triangular pyramids so that each five meet at the points marked with a star in the illustration

30-unit assembly with closed petals

Passiflora Delicata ✳✳✳

PAPER: Use a 7–10 cm (2 ¾–4 inches) square for each unit

NUMBER OF UNITS: 12 or 30

This model has very long delicate petals, which can be arranged in various ways. Use your imagination to create your very own special flower.

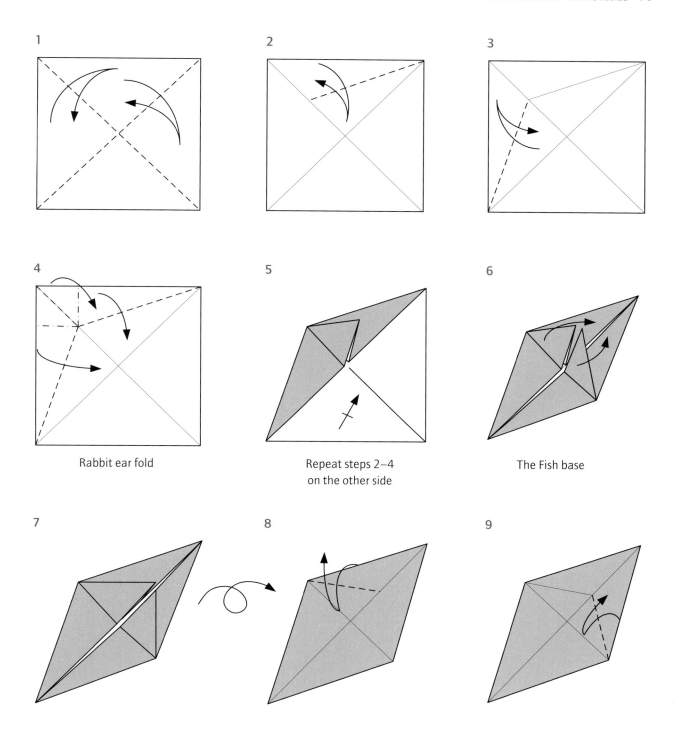

1

2

3

4

Rabbit ear fold

5

Repeat steps 2–4
on the other side

6

The Fish base

7

8

9

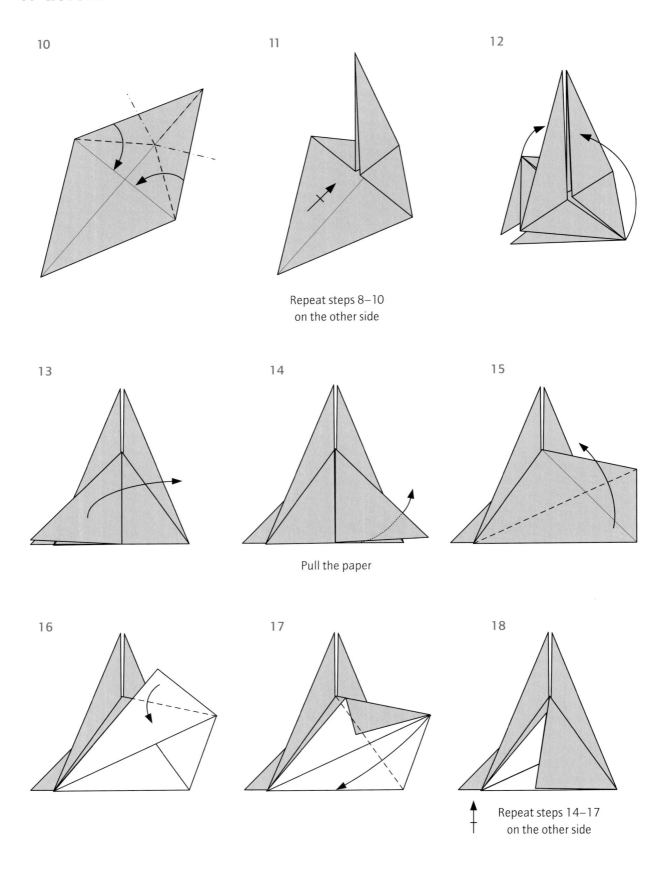

10

11

Repeat steps 8–10
on the other side

12

13

14

Pull the paper

15

16

17

18

Repeat steps 14–17
on the other side

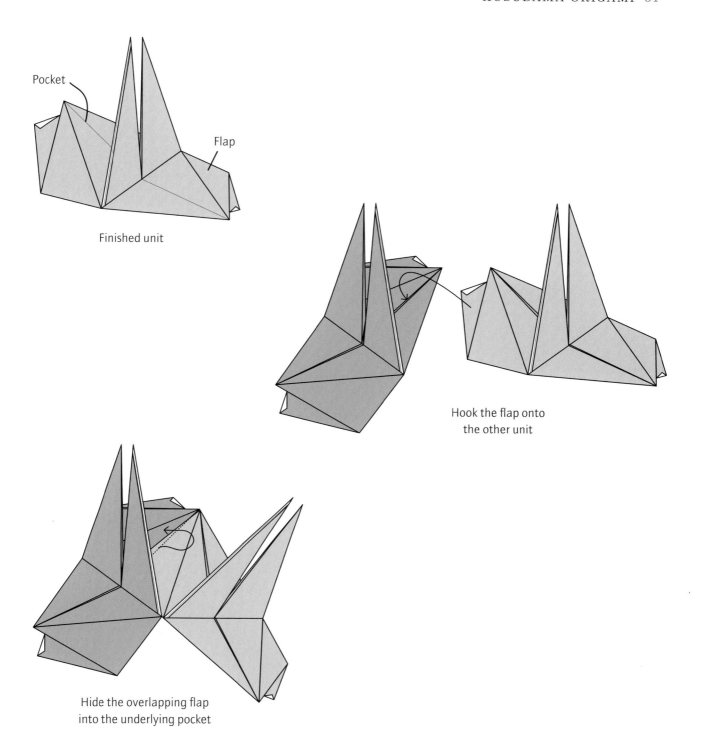

Pocket

Flap

Finished unit

Hook the flap onto
the other unit

Hide the overlapping flap
into the underlying pocket

12-UNIT ASSEMBLY: use the assembly method on page 76

30-UNIT ASSEMBLY: use the assembly method on page 77

Passiflora Bicolor ✳✳✳✳

PAPER: **Use a 7–10 cm (2¾–4 inches) square for each unit**

NUMBER OF UNITS: **12 or 30**

This model has long asymmetric petals. Use duo paper to get the best results.

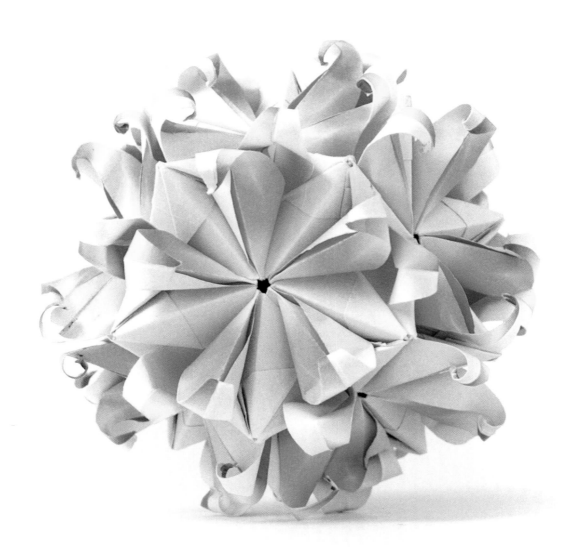

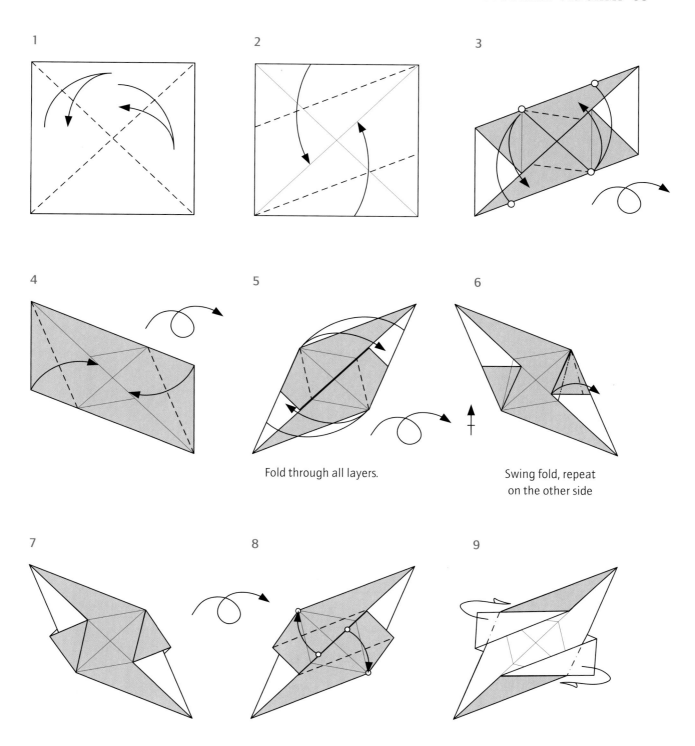

Fold through all layers.

Swing fold, repeat
on the other side

10

11

12

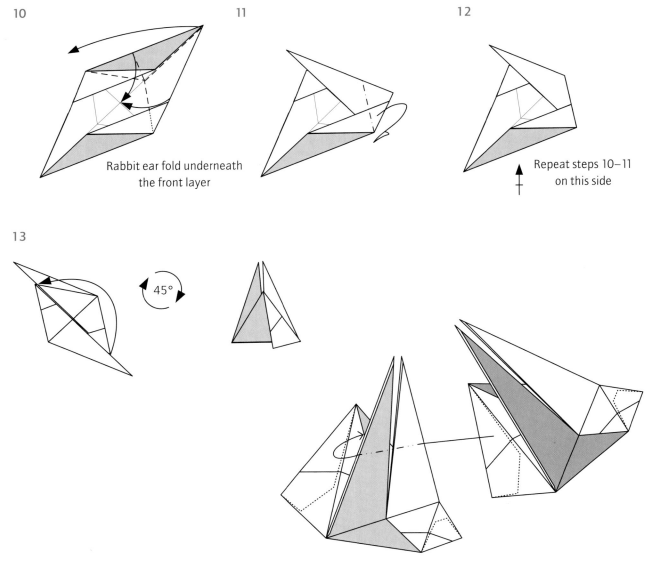

Rabbit ear fold underneath
the front layer

Repeat steps 10–11
on this side

13

45°

Hook one unit onto another

12-UNIT ASSEMBLY: use the assembly method on page 76

30-UNIT ASSEMBLY: use the assembly method on page 77

Passiflora Rhombica ✳✳

PAPER: Use a 7–10 cm (2¾–4 inches) square for each unit

NUMBER OF UNITS: 12 or 30

The model has small flowers "growing" between the pyramids. By inserting little squares of other colors into the units you can get plenty of color variations, even if you only use plain paper.

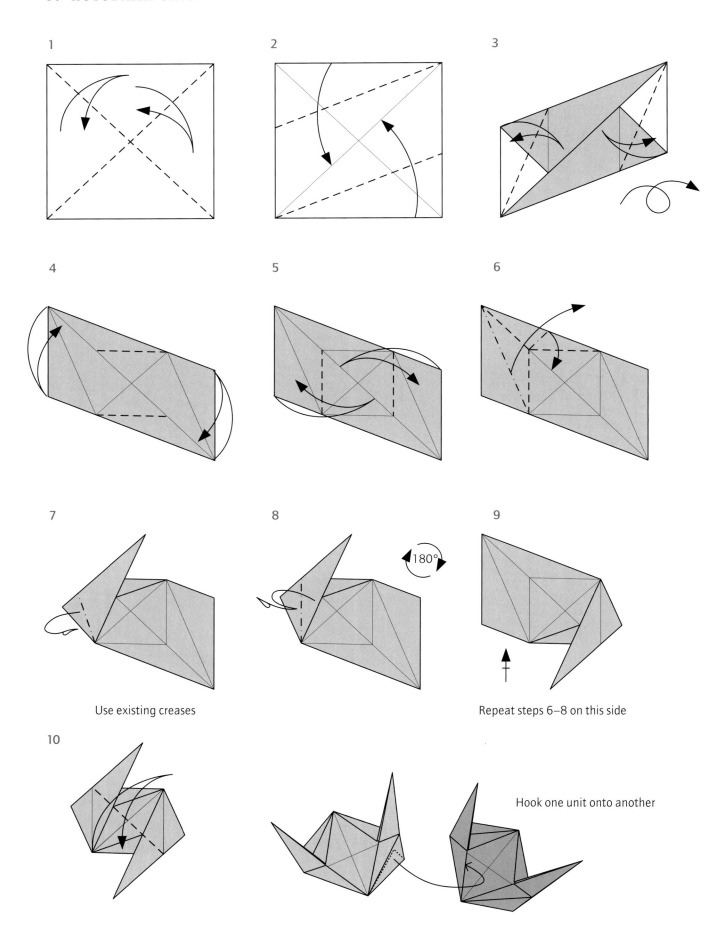

1

2

3

4

5

6

7

Use existing creases

8

180°

9

Repeat steps 6–8 on this side

10

Hook one unit onto another

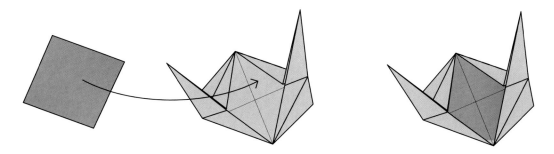

Hint: put a small square of paper of a different color inside each unit and get plenty of color effects.

12-UNIT ASSEMBLY

Form 4 triangular pyramids around every point
marked with a star as in the illustrations

30-UNIT ASSEMBLY

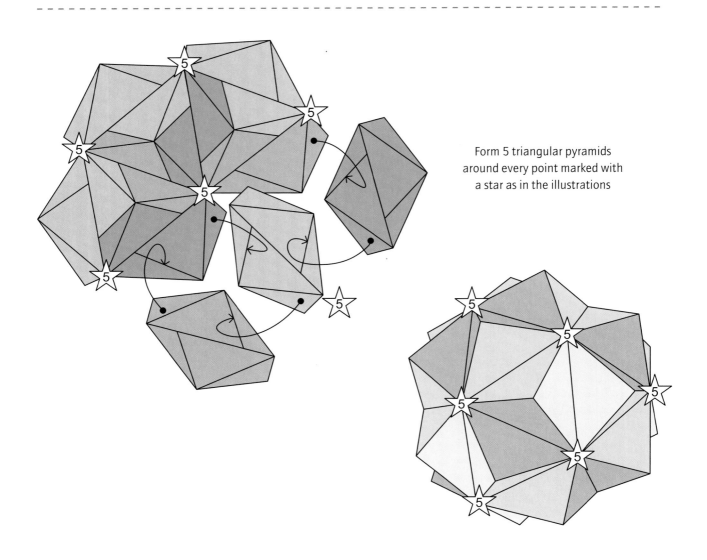

Form 5 triangular pyramids around every point marked with a star as in the illustrations

Passiflora Ornata ✳✳✳

PAPER: Use a 7–10 cm (2¾–4 inches) square for each unit

NUMBER OF UNITS: 12 or 30

This model has small, two-colored flowers between the pyramids. Use duo paper for the best results.

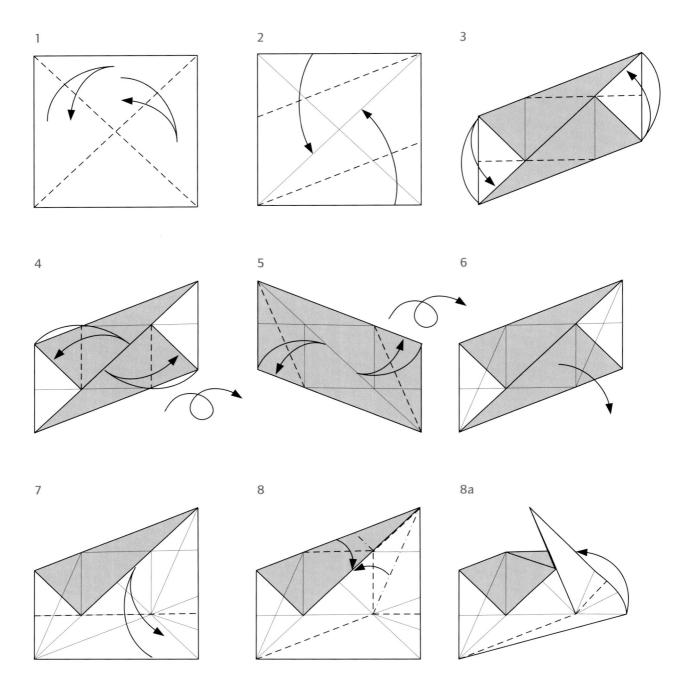

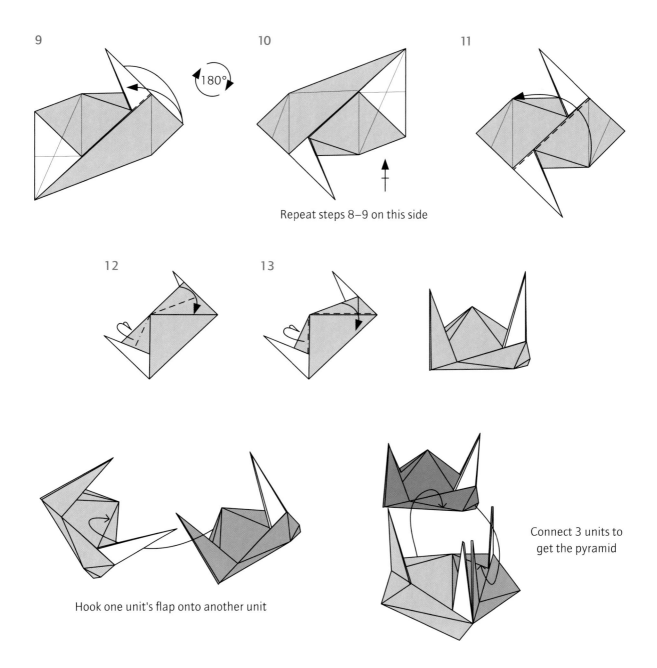

9

10

180°

Repeat steps 8–9 on this side

11

12

13

Hook one unit's flap onto another unit

Connect 3 units to get the pyramid

12-UNIT ASSEMBLY: use the assembly method on page 87

30-UNIT ASSEMBLY: use the assembly method on page 88

Passiflora Ornata with Spirals ✳✳✳

- -

PAPER: **Use a 9–12 cm (3½–4¾ inches) square for each unit**

NUMBER OF UNITS: **12**

This is the cube with pretty spirals on the sides. Use three or more colors for this model to make the spirals contrast.

11

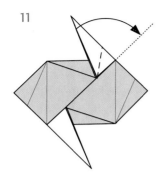

Start with step 11 of the
Passiflora Ornata unit

12

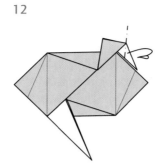

13

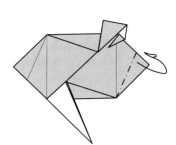

14

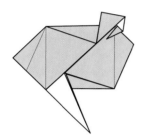

15

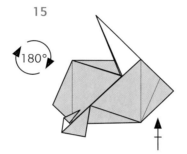

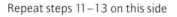

Repeat steps 11–13 on this side

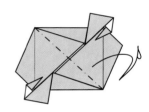

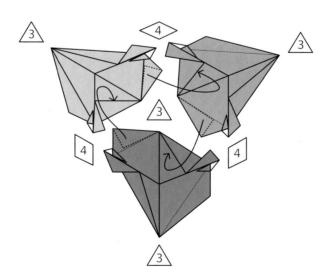

Hook one unit onto another using the flap. Then hook the parts of
the spiral onto each other. Connect 3 units at one point as shown.
Add other units to form a cube. Each face of the cube is formed
with 4 units. Each vertex of the cube is formed with 3 units.

Mosaic **

PAPER: Use paper with 2:3 side proportions. For example, 4 x 6 cm (1 ½ x 2 ¼ inches), 6 x 9 cm (2 ¼ x 3 3/8 inches) or larger are sizes that work well. See page xiii for how to cut this rectangle from a square.

NUMBER OF UNITS: 12 or 30. The most beautiful result can be achieved using 30 units.

Use duo paper for this model and you'll get a pretty patterned ball. You can experiment with colors and get a variety of multi-colored balls.

1

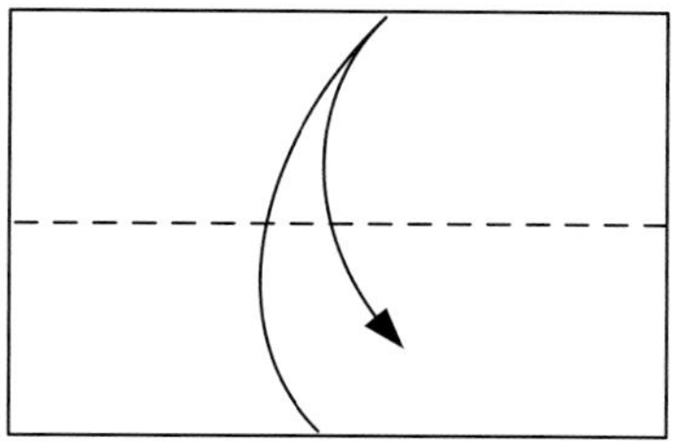

2:3 rectangle

2

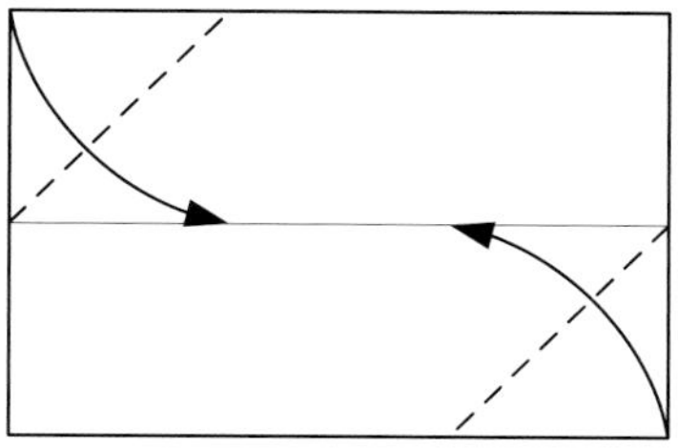

3

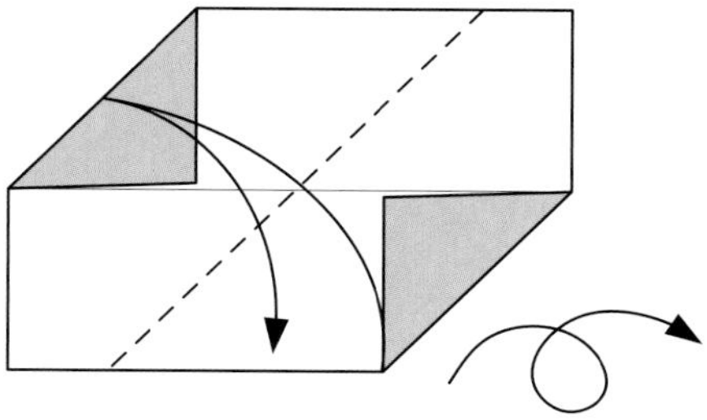

4

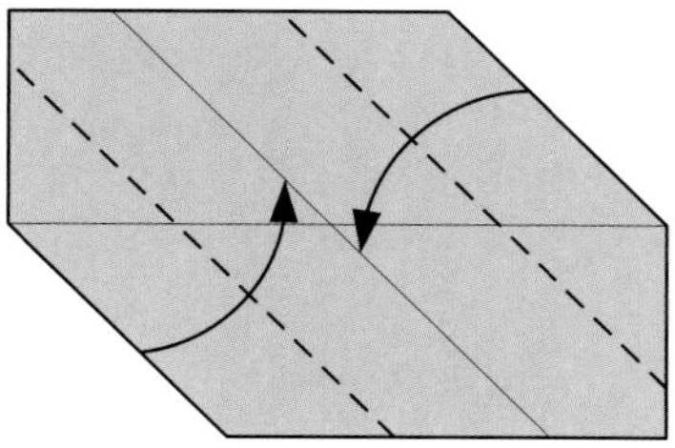

5

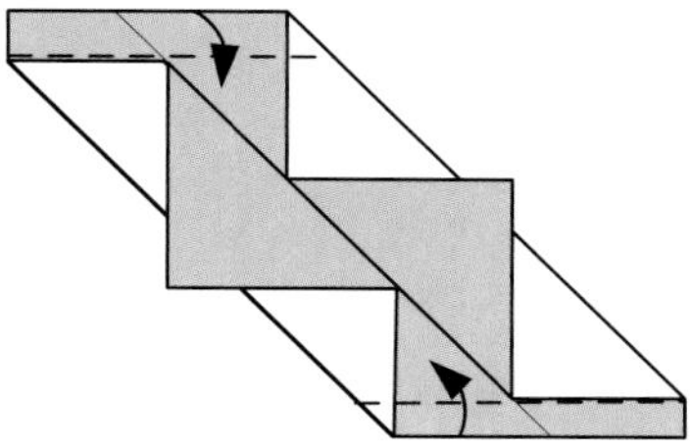

6

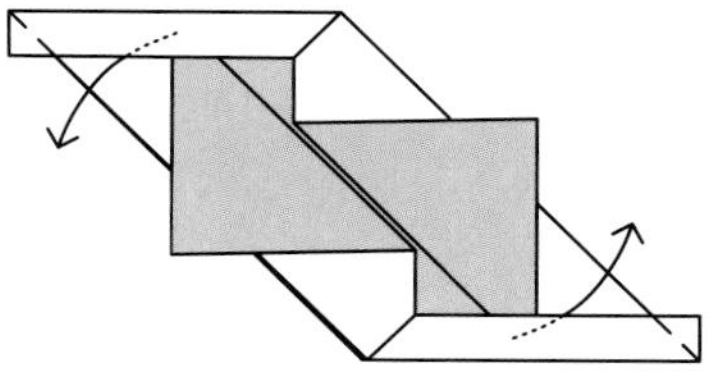

Release the layers

7

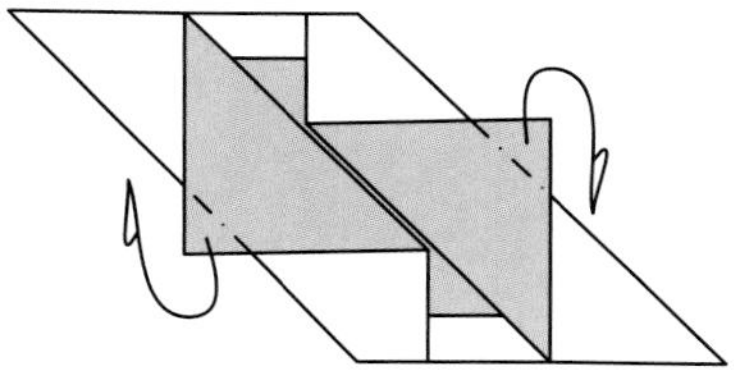

8

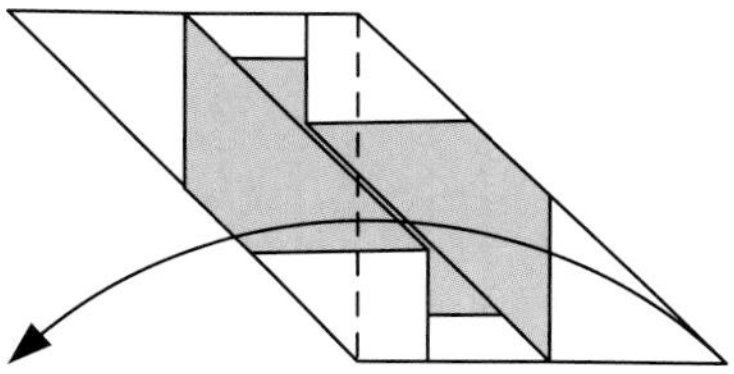

9

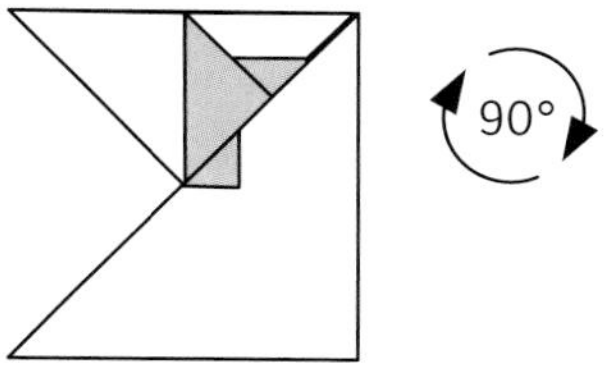

90°

10

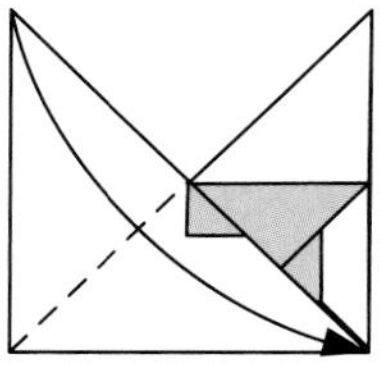

11

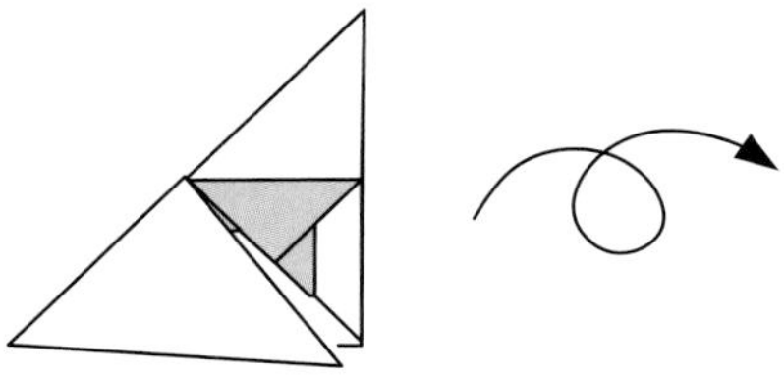

12

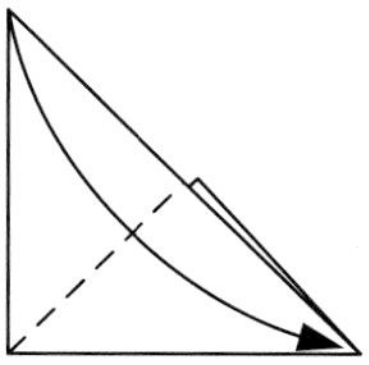

Open the unit a bit

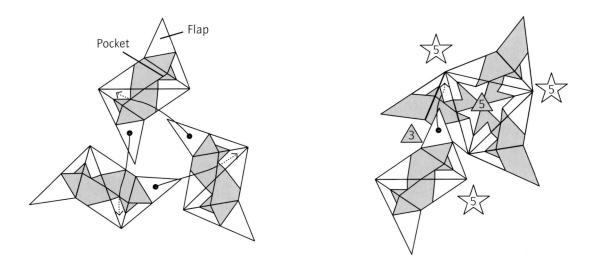

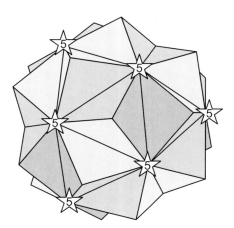

Assemble every 3 units into a pyramid as shown. Add other units so that 5 pyramids meet in the points, marked with the stars in the illustration.

Thunderbolt ✳ ✳

PAPER: Use paper with 2:3 side proportions. For example, 4 x 6 cm (1½ x 2 ¼ inches), 6 x 9 cm (2 ¼ x 3 ⅜ inches), or larger would work well. See page xiv for how to cut this rectangle from a square.

NUMBER OF UNITS: 12 or 30. The most beautiful result can be obtained by using 30 units.

Use duo paper for this model and you'll get the symbol of a thunderbolt in the faces of each spike. Start with step 5 of the Mosaic unit.

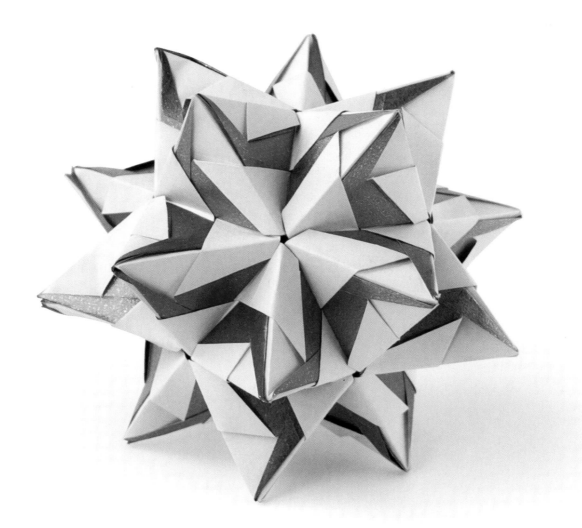

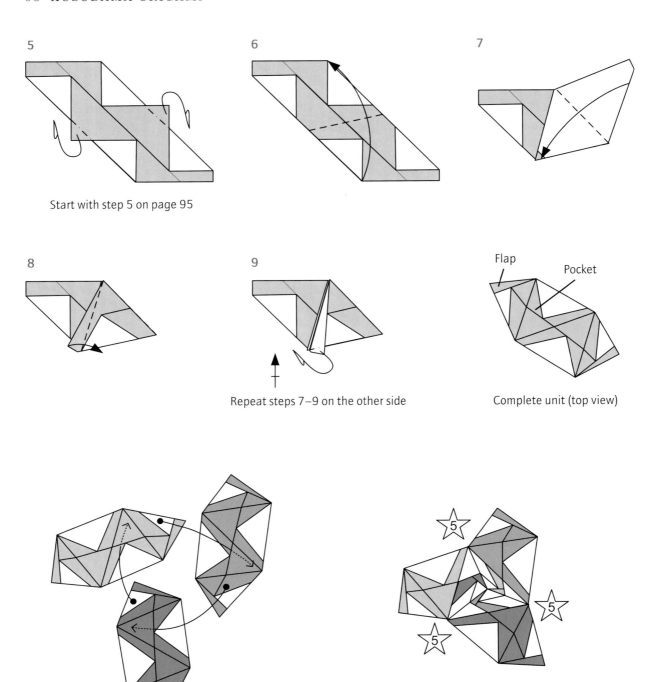

5

Start with step 5 on page 95

6

7

8

9

Repeat steps 7–9 on the other side

Flap

Pocket

Complete unit (top view)

Assemble 3 units to a pyramid. Form triangular pyramids each time so that 5 pyramids meet at the points marked with the stars in the illustration.

12-UNIT ASSEMBLY: use the assembly method on page 76

30-UNIT ASSEMBLY: use the assembly method on page 77

Benjamin ✳✳✳

PAPER: Use U.S. banknotes. If you are not that rich, you can use a rectangle with the proportions ~1:2.3 or see page xiv for how to cut this rectangle from a square. I recommend rectangles about 6 x 13.8 cm (2¼ x 5⅜ inches) or larger.

NUMBER OF UNITS: 12 or 30

You can use this as a valuable gift or as a piggy bank. But… don't glue the units together!

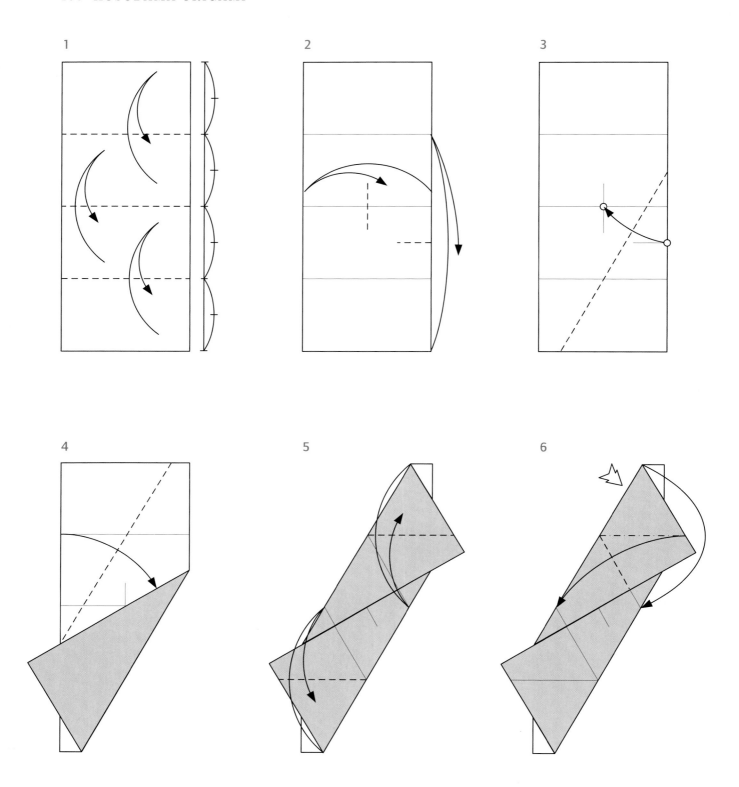

7

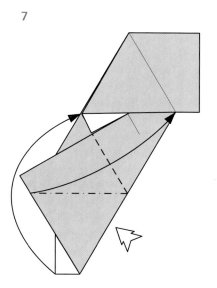

8

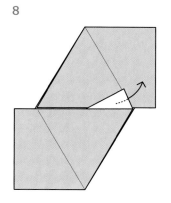

Pull the paper from underneath

9

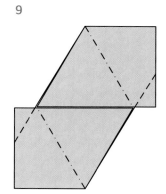

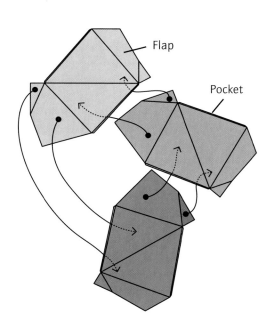

Flap

Pocket

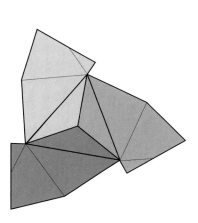

12-UNIT ASSEMBLY: use the assembly method on page 76

30-UNIT ASSEMBLY: use the assembly method on page 77

Precious ✳✳✳

- -

PAPER: Use U.S. banknotes. If you are not that rich, you can use a rectangle with the proportion ~1:2.3, or See page xivfor how to cut this rectangle from a square. I recommend rectangles approximately 6 x 13.8 cm (2¼ x 5⅜ inches) or larger.

NUMBER OF UNITS: 4, 12, or 30

If you use real banknotes, this can become a really precious spike. I must say that U.S.-dollar paper is one of the best papers for modular origami I've ever tried. Unfortunately the models for this book were made with fake bills. But when I become rich…

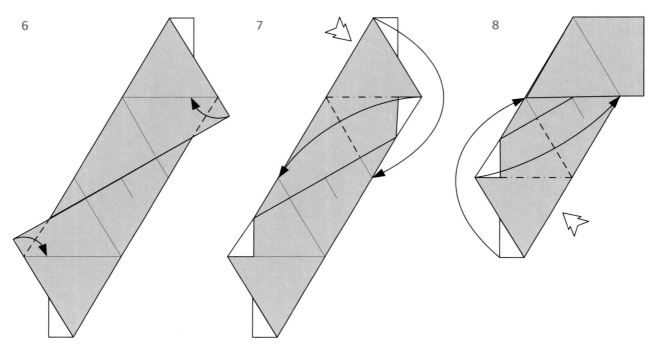

Start with step 6 of the Benjamin model

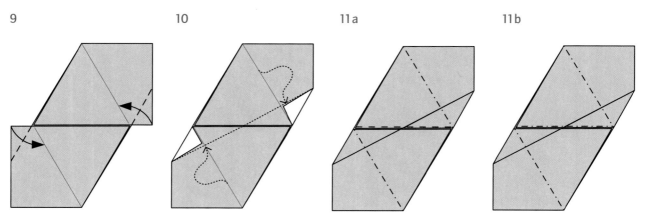

Rearrange layers

The direction of the center fold depends on the unit type you want to achieve. Use unit "type A" for 12- or 30-unit assembly, and unit "type B" for 4-unit assembly.

CONNECTING DOUBLE-POCKET UNITS

To connect two units, put one flap into a pocket and another flap into another pocket at the same time. It's a bit tricky, but you get a very strong connection.

You can create two types of the unit. Unit type A is assembled to a spike (see pages 76 and 77). Unit type B can be assembled into a 4-unit octahedron (see page 106).

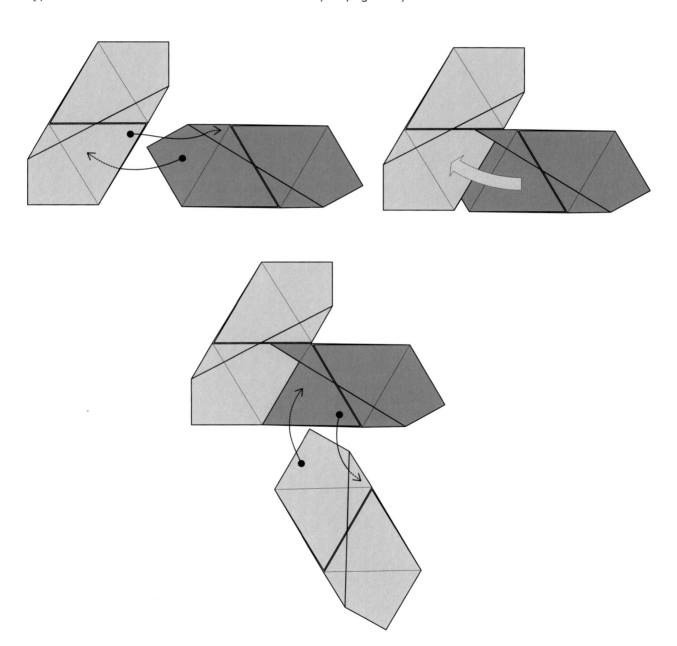

If you alter the folds in step 9, you get plenty of ornament combinations:

VARIATION A

9

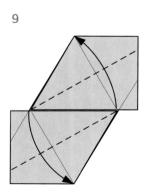

Start at step 9 of unit on page 102

10

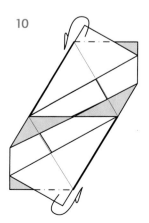

11a

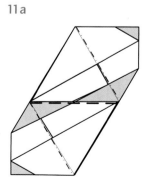

See page 103, "Connecting
double-pocket units" for
help with connection

VARIATION B

9

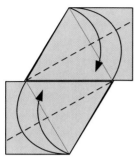

Start at step 9 of unit on page 102

10

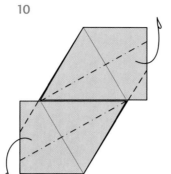

Rearrange layers

11

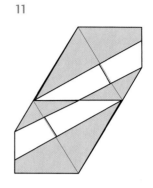

See page 103, "Connecting double-pocket units" for help with connection

VARIATION C

9

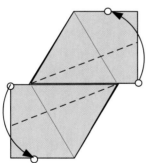

Start at step 9 of unit on page 102

10

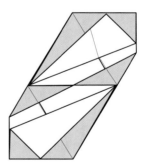

See page 103, "Connecting double-pocket units" for help with connection

4-UNIT OCTAHEDRON ASSEMBLY

Unit type B assembly

Connect 4 units of type B into a pyramid, then connect the other sides of the units at the back. All points marked with the stars meet at one point.

Lucky Star ✳✳✳

PAPER: You can use any sized rectangle as long as it has dimensions in a 1:x ratio, where 1.15 < x < 2.3. The only restriction is that you should use the same size rectangle for each of the units in the model. The diagrams are given for 1:2 rectangles, but you can adjust the same steps below to other rectangles. I recommend using rectangles about 7 cm (2¾ inches) in width.

NUMBER OF UNITS: 12 or 30

30-unit assembly is recommended if you want to get pretty stars between the spikes.

1

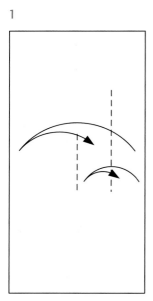

Take a rectangle of any size (the diagram
is for the 1:2 rectangle but the same
steps can be applied to ones with other
dimensions—1:X where X<2.3)

2

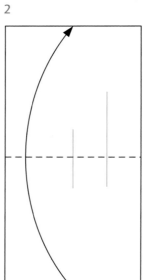

3

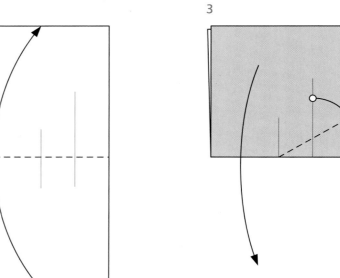

4

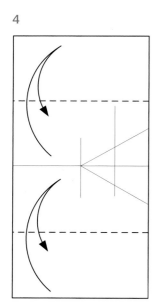

5

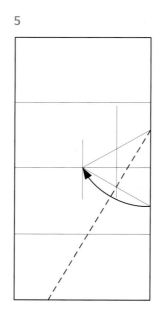

6

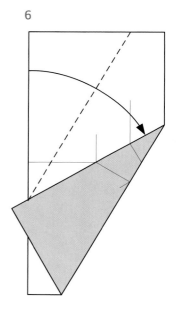

7

8

9

Repeat the same
on the other side

10

11

Reverse fold inside, repeat
on the other side

12

12-UNIT ASSEMBLY: use the assembly method on page 76

30-UNIT ASSEMBLY: use the assembly method on page 77

You can also use the following method: Connect 3 units as shown. Add other units so that the pentagonal holes appear in the model (they are marked with stars in the illustration below). Three units should meet at the places marked with triangles each time. See picture of the complete model for reference.

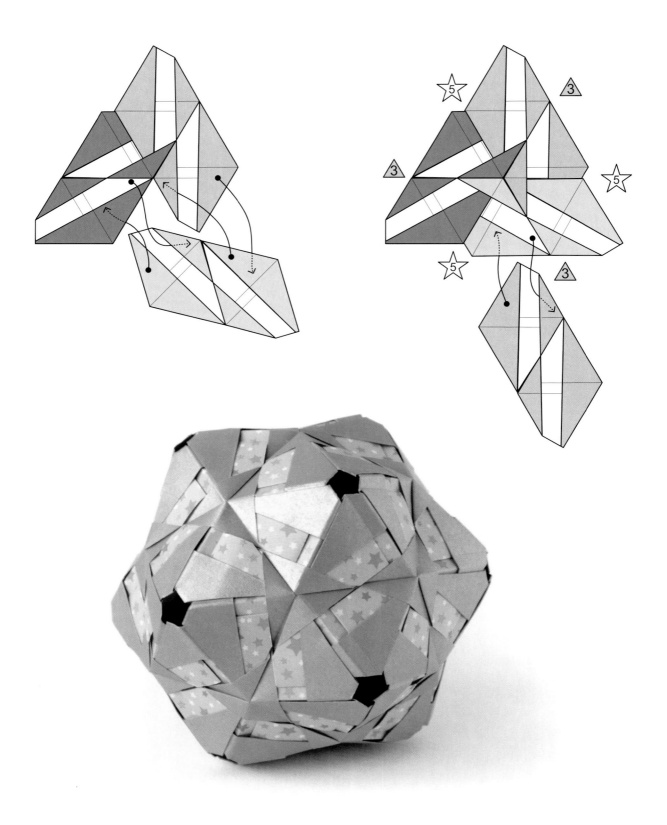

Life Inside ✳✳✳✳

PAPER: Use a 7–10 cm (2¾–4 inches) square for each unit.

NUMBER OF UNITS: 30

Curl the flaps of this model and you get a beautiful floral ball.

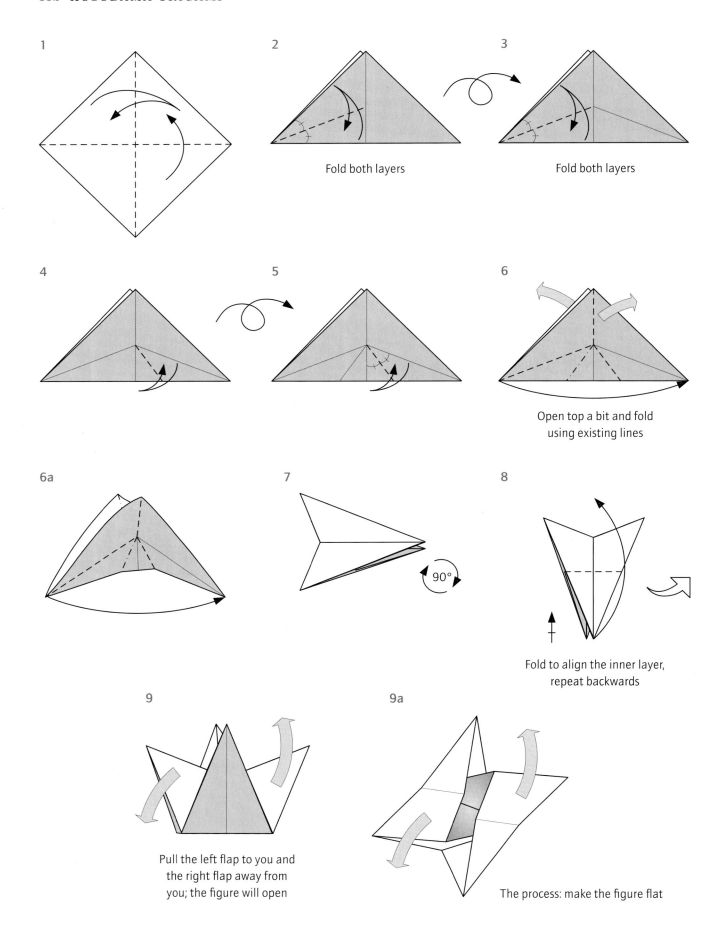

1

2
Fold both layers

3
Fold both layers

4

5

6
Open top a bit and fold
using existing lines

6a

7
90°

8
Fold to align the inner layer,
repeat backwards

9
Pull the left flap to you and
the right flap away from
you; the figure will open

9a
The process: make the figure flat

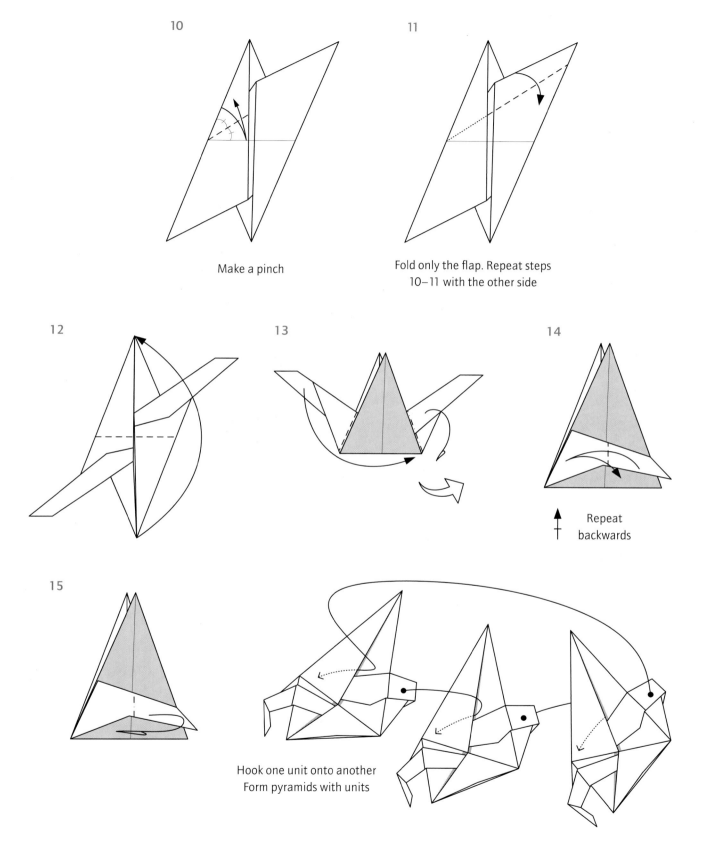

10

Make a pinch

11

Fold only the flap. Repeat steps
10–11 with the other side

12

13

14

↑ Repeat
backwards

15

Hook one unit onto another
Form pyramids with units

30-UNIT ASSEMBLY: use the assembly method on page 77

About the Author

In trying to write something about myself, I understand that my life may seem rather dull from an outsider's viewpoint. Since very early childhood I was so fascinated with mind games—with puzzles, construction sets, beautiful books about art and architecture—that I had no time nor hunger for physical adventure. I was a rather good girl. I studied hard and entered a good university. Initially I wanted to become an architect or a designer, but I became a mathematician. Why? Now I think it was fate. During my studies I worked as a volunteer in a student organization.

After that I became a postgraduate student. I still don't know why; maybe because I like to study. I recently defended my thesis in mathematics. I still don't understand how I managed it! All I can say is, inventing origami models is much less effort and gives me fewer headaches than math!

I'm married and work as a programmer now. Life isn't dull at all! It is always interesting, and I am never bored. I have plenty of hobbies: I like to draw, model, plant cactuses, and work in the garden. And of course do origami. Every moment is interesting if you know how to enjoy it!

WHY ORIGAMI?

Why did I choose origami among other creative hobbies? The only answer I can think of is that I adore puzzles. And they challenge your brain only until you solve them. After that you can throw them away! Most of the conundrums have only one solution. A blank sheet of paper has infinite possibilities. You can fold it either into an animal or into a modular. Even if you solve one puzzle, there exist thousands more!

Origami is also very relaxing. For me it's even a bit meditative. You fold, fold, and fold and all of your other problems move to the background.

HOW ORIGAMI?

I'm usually questioned about how I create. The answer is easy, but it's hard to understand. Peter Engel[1] discussed the "psychology of invention," the thought processes that lead to invention. I totally agree with him. In short, you think over some problem or question. If the solution is not immediately evident you may start thinking about something else, or even not think at all. But your subconscious still thinks over that problem. The solution can suddenly come to you when you are lying on the sofa or even sleeping. It may flash through your mind with a cry of "Eureka!" That's what happens with me. I invented most of my best models with my subconscious. Sometimes I was even slumbering during this process. You just have to wake up at the right moment. It's easy, but it's also hard to understand; you have to feel it.

But that's not all. After catching the idea from the air, I work it over. I search for ways to implement this new idea (for example how to connect the units) to various origami forms or previously made models. You can obtain something new and interesting by combining several ideas. Sometimes I feel like a selectionist that cross-breeds new sorts of flowers.

[1] Peter Engel. *Origami from Angelfish to Zen*. New York: Dover Publications, Inc., 1994, p. 66.